T0355837

AN END TO
INEQUALITY

Also by Jonathan Kozol

Death at an Early Age

The Night Is Dark and I Am Far from Home

Illiterate America

Rachel and Her Children

Savage Inequalities

Amazing Grace

Ordinary Resurrections

The Shame of the Nation

Letters to a Young Teacher

Fire in the Ashes

The Theft of Memory

AN END TO INEQUALITY

Breaking Down the Walls of Apartheid Education in America

JONATHAN KOZOL

NEW YORK
LONDON

Requests for permission to reproduce selections from this book should be
made through our website: https://thenewpress.com/contact.

Published in the United States by The New Press, New York, 2024

Distributed by Two Rivers Distribution

ISBN 978-1-62097-872-6 (hc)
ISBN 978-1-62097-875-7 (ebook)
CIP data is available

The New Press publishes books that promote and enrich public discussion and understanding
of the issues vital to our democracy and to a more equitable world. These books are made
possible by the enthusiasm of our readers; the support of a committed group of donors, large
and small; the collaboration of our many partners in the independent media and the not-for-
profit sector; booksellers, who often hand-sell New Press books; librarians; and above all by
our authors.

www.thenewpress.com

Composition by Dix Digital Prepress and Design
This book was set in Adobe Garamond Pro

Printed in the United States of America

2 4 6 8 10 9 7 5 3 1

For Jean McGuire,
with the deepest gratitude
for all the glorious years
of struggle in which
we've worked together

But the day will come—
You are sure yourselves that it is coming—
When the marching feet of the masses
Will raise for you a living monument of love,
And joy, and laughter,
And black hands and white hands clasped as one,
And a song that reaches the sky. . . .
                                        —Langston Hughes

Contents

Foreword

For more than fifty years, Jonathan Kozol has been shining a light on the dark corners of racially separate and financially unequal education in American public schools. He never succumbed to the cynicism and racism that led so many Americans to betray the promise of *Brown v. Board of Education*. Even while, in American jurisprudence, *Brown* is hallowed but hollow, Kozol's crusade for bringing our children together in their classrooms has never wavered.

I have always thought the title of Jonathan's first book, *Death at an Early Age*, vividly captured the lives and experiences of many of my childhood friends from public housing projects like the one in which I grew up in the Bronx, and from segregated schools and neighborhoods throughout the country. Too many lived abbreviated lives, cut short by drugs, violence, and opportunities denied. But just as tragically, too many had their intellectual lives snuffed out by the savagely unequal education they were given in their public schools.

In the culminating work of a remarkable career, Jonathan recounts the rigid and mechanical way in which segregated Black schools prioritize discipline and punishment over intellectual curiosity and creativity. In recent years, many public school systems have hired corporate executives, lawyers, or retired military officers to run schools or administer entire districts. But it is not solely a matter of who oversees education; school systems have adopted corporate or military paradigms, supposedly in the interest of efficiency.

Corporal punishment, an especially Southern phenomenon, is particularly disturbing. Jonathan reminds us that the U.S. Supreme Court ruled in 1977 that corporal punishment in public schools does not violate the Constitution. Still, he asks, is it a coincidence that corporal punishment is most common in the regions of the country stamped by slavery and Jim Crow segregation—and that Black and brown children are disproportionately subjected to this punishment?

Many of Kozol's examples of corporal punishment are nothing less than instances of brutality, and he calls it out for what it is: "The states and counties where lynchings were most common are those in which Black and Latino children are most likely to experience these physical transgressions at the hands of school officials." Kozol writes of Black and brown children, sometimes as young as six or eight years old, who are criminalized in public schools that have become pathways to the prison system. He also writes of schools characterized by squalor and dysfunctional facilities. Of the students who attend these schools, he writes, "Squalor and decrepitude soil their mentalities."

The physical degradation these children undergo echoes

the conditions in racially segregated public schools prior to *Brown*. These separate and unequal schools are no longer mandated by law, but they are, nonetheless, sanctioned and permitted by the law.

Kozol highlights a possible lawsuit, proposed by civil rights attorneys, that would "build a bridge between Boston's mostly Black and brown students and their mostly white and Asian peers in the suburbs." But in 1974, in *Milliken v. Bradley*, the Supreme Court erected almost insurmountable obstacles to the pursuit of school desegregation in the federal courts, thus leaving all-Black school systems surrounded by white suburban schools as a hallmark of American metropolitan areas. And the court has also ruled that school funding based on local property value that replicates economic inequalities between school districts were not constitutionally cognizable or justiciable (*San Antonio v. Rodriguez* in 1973). Taken together, *Rodriguez* and *Milliken* leave racially separate and financially unequal public schools beyond the reach of federal law.

Thus, Black students are legally in a worse position than they were under *Plessy*, when at least in theory they were entitled to equally funded, even if racially segregated, schools. While the lawsuit to which Kozol alludes is unlikely to be feasible in federal court, state courts offer us some hope. In some cases, state-level litigation, seeking to enforce educational adequacy, "thorough and efficient education," or other clauses in state constitutions (for example, Massachusetts, North Carolina, and New York) has met with limited success, leading to some liability decisions but rarely to meaningful remedial orders.

Tired of chasing white people and rejecting the spurious notion that their children must sit next to white children in order to learn, many Black people have given up on the idea of school desegregation and would opt for adequately funded schools and community control. Yet segregated schools have never worked well for most African American students, not because all-Black institutions are *per se* inferior, but because segregation has always been accompanied by other forms of organized injustice.

Most white Americans, as evidenced by their unwilling-ness to enroll their children in schools with large numbers of Black and brown students, have never embraced the promise of *Brown*. Kozol correctly asserts that parents of white students have had no problem with school bus transportation to bring their children to their local school. "Busing" became a pejorative term only when the bus was bringing children of color to those schools. Many white Americans purport to honor *Brown* and the idea of integration, but too often they do so only in principle—for other people's children, not their own.

Jonathan Kozol is a rarity. He taught at a segregated public school in Boston in the decade following *Brown*. He believed in the intellectual potential of the children in his fourth grade class and struggled to help them overcome the miserable conditions that they faced. Almost six decades later, he remains an unrelenting advocate for school desegregation. He also points to voluntary and successful inter-district integration programs in which he has been personally involved. The Boston-area Metco program is one such success story with a long history, and Jonathan describes the experience of dozens of children he has known who have flourished in the program and have since gone on to college and rewarding adult lives.

Jonathan will no doubt be criticized, as he has been before, by those who believe that the educational failures and shortcomings of Black students are the consequences of familial pathology and individual failures of responsibility. These critics deny the existence and importance of structural and institutionalized racism. They have been staunch opponents of school desegregation and will continue to see his strong convictions to be anathema to the policies and practices they defend. Just as Jonathan was fired by the Boston schools for teaching Black students a Langston Hughes poem long ago, these critics will doubtless try to silence him again. But, if it is true that we are known by the enemies we make, Jonathan Kozol remains in good company. He has walked with and among the great civil rights leaders and advocates of America.

In an eloquent passage, Jonathan pays tribute to John Lewis, whom I was also blessed to know. I resist the notion that, given his age, Jonathan does not believe he will live to see the day when we as a nation summon up the will "to batter down the walls that make our children strangers to each other," but I suspect that it is no less true for me. Still, we will struggle on together and we will pray that the younger generation of advocates and activists will continue in that struggle to make our nation whole. I hope that this timely and urgent and important book will help to spur them on.

> Theodore M. Shaw
> Julius L. Chambers Distinguished Professor of Law
> University of North Carolina School of Law and
> Director of UNC Center for Civil Rights
> Chapel Hill, NC

To the Reader

In writing this book, I have drawn upon visits I have made to a wide array of elementary schools over the course of the recent fifteen years. The names and identities of principals and teachers are usually disguised—and the schools in which they work are generally not named—in order to protect their privacy. In a very few cases, I identify a school, but only when the name in itself has particular significance or is included in a document I'm citing. Documentation for all statistics and matters of public record cited in these pages is provided in the Endnotes, which begin on page 145.

AN END TO
INEQUALITY

1

Two Degrees of Separation

For more than half a century, I've been working with young children and their teachers in schools that serve low-income Black and brown communities and, in my books, I've underscored repeatedly the nearly total isolation of these children from the mainstream of American society. School segregation, as we know, continues unabated and is presently at its highest level since the early 1990s. The ruling of the Warren court in *Brown v. Board of Education* is like a ghost of Christmas past. Its legacy and spirit have largely been abandoned.

But segregation, in and of itself, is not the primary subject of this book. We are dealing today not only with a physical divide that is obvious to anyone who spends much time in public schools, but also with a parallel divide between two worlds of pedagogic practice and methods of instructional control: one of them a tightly wired code of discipline and training that is held to be appropriate for children of one class and race, the other with more space and time for children to take some joy in learning as an act of exploration.

The notion that young children of color need a uniquely different course of training than white children because of their allegedly inherent liabilities, or liabilities attributed to parental "failings," has always been a subtext in arguments presented by those who see no merit in school desegregation and was often heard in Boston when I was in my first year as a teacher in 1964 and 1965. I later described the open expression of these views in the words of school officials when I published *Death at an Early Age* about the school where I was teaching. I was a young and naïve optimist. I wanted to think that these beliefs would dissipate in time and would be consigned at last to the trash heap of our racist history.

It turns out I was wrong. Over the course of recent decades, these ideas have surfaced once again and have been elaborately revitalized and reified and seemingly legitimized by influential figures at conservative foundations as well as by their counterparts at many universities. School officials in all too many of our urban districts often appear to share the same perceptions of the students in their classrooms.

According to this thinking, Black and Latino children have different ways of understanding what we should expect of them than white and middle-class children do. They come to us, as we've been told, with troubled minds and unruly temperaments that cannot be subdued by normal forms of discipline. Different needs require different strategies. The strategy in this case, as I began to hear the latest iteration of this argument emerging, includes a wide array of practices intended to revise the sensibilities of children and to militate against the indulgence of their youthful curiosities, in order to keep them on a straight gray line of march to their next examination. Sitting stiff and silent in the classroom, no impulsive and unscripted questions, many numbered lists of minor misbehaviors and the unpleasant penalties for each, regimens of shaming for those who aren't "performing up to expectations"—all of these are pieces of the disparate agenda.

So long as it's accepted that these are the most productive strategies for governing the temperaments of children of a different class and color, any serious attempt at racial integration of our public schools would seem to be foolhardy—and would, indeed, run counter to the interests of those children, as their interests are perceived by those who really do believe they come to us in kindergarten or first grade, or preschool for that matter, as deficient little people. Why go to all the trouble it would take to let them go to schools where six-year-olds can move around the room and scrunch their legs up on their chairs and do not have to live in fear of penalties for looking out the window or whispering or laughing when they think that something's funny? Why allow them this degree of normal informality, and this opportunity to interact with kids who come from other backgrounds and other racial origins, if all of this is contraindicated by "the data that we have in hand," as we are told so frequently?

It's not surprising that the right-leaning institutes in

Washington and elsewhere have aggressively promoted these beliefs. These are the same forces, or the latter-day descendants of those forces, that promoted voucher schemes and separatist academies in Southern states in efforts to resist the integration struggles and the rulings of the courts in the days when Dr. King and Thurgood Marshall were alive. The real heartbreaker is that so many otherwise enlightened people appear to find these arguments convincing—or, at least, convenient rationales for leaving poor Black and Latino children where they are, "over there," in schools that can deliver what they "need." Would it not be a disservice to these children, according to this logic, to bring them into schools in which the special medicine that's been prescribed for them is simply not available?

This is a book about that "special medicine"—the targeting of children, on the basis of their economic status and skin color, with a brand of education that is crudely autocratic and, in the worst of cases that I've seen, grimly reminiscent of the Era of Eugenics. At a time when democratic values are under fierce assault, too little has been said about this clearly racialized agenda. One class of children is given at least some random opportunities to ask discerning questions, to interrogate everyday realities, and their teachers are not cautioned to suppress and penalize every indication of their often justifiable and serious or sometimes simply whimsical irreverence.

Another class of children is not to be permitted the same luxuries.

The idea of a different breed of child who learns and feels and comprehends in wholly different ways than the children of the experts who have drawn this demarcation is an ignorant and dangerous construction. It widens the gulf between the favored and the disempowered. It inculcates unquestioning conformity. It closes the window on the full capaciousness of learning. It does not build on the richness of Black culture or any mix of cultures. It isn't about culture. It's about containment. It isn't good for children, and it's not good for America.

2

Varieties of Tyranny

In a nation with nearly 100,000 public schools in almost 14,000 districts, there are obviously plenty of exceptions to the pattern I've described. Dozens of principals and hundreds of teachers who invite me to their schools do not accept the arguments that underpin and justify the disparate agenda and refuse to swallow the idea that children of color are uniquely different in their ways of understanding than any other children in America.

Still, determined efforts have been made to convince the teachers in far too many schools that serve Black and Latino children—and this is especially the case with young and newly hired teachers—to steer away from normal and good-natured informality in the ways they act and even in the choice of words they use in speaking to their students. An entire lexicon of warnings and commandments has been developed and promoted in the training of these teachers.

"Scholar position!" the teacher says in a coded formula I've heard in several schools. "Tractor beams! One, two, three! Eyes on me. Zero talk." If the child talks or looks away, tell her she's in "red zone."

"Scholar position" means that you must sit up straight, hands together, palm to palm. "Tractor beams" means your

eyes are fixed intently on the teacher. "Red zone" is a warning code. It means you're in the highest range of incorrect
behavior.

How do you persuade a teacher with a healthy personality
who comes to education with a fondness for young children
to talk like this to students? In many districts it begins by
putting teachers into programs of re-training, frequently provided by purported experts from private sector groups that
contract with the school systems to toughen up the atmosphere of learning and modify the style of the teachers.

A teacher in low-income Lawrence, Massachusetts, where
children of color, many of them from Dominican and Puerto
Rican families, make up ninety-six percent of public school
enrollment, is told by an observer from a teacher-training
corporation, who is sitting with two other trainers in the
back row of her sixth grade classroom, that she's smiling too
much at her students—"I came across as too happy," she was
told—and wasn't standing stiff enough and straight enough
while talking to her children. According to the teacher, whose
story got some brief attention in 2015 when it was cited by
Valerie Strauss in her blog in The Washington Post, "I was
told to stand in 'mountain pose' and not to favor one leg over
another. I was told not to cross my legs. My body language
must be in no way casual. . . ." She was also told her tone of

voice conveyed too much enthusiasm and that she was giving children too much praise when they did a lesson right or
behaved correctly.

The teacher-training experts were speaking to the teacher
through an ear-piece that she had to wear and which, of
course, the children noticed and which, she said, they found
perplexing. "Miss," a student asked her, "what's that in your
ear?" When another of the students spoke up out of turn, she
was told through her ear-piece, "Give him a warning." When
the boy kept talking, "Tell him he has a detention."

At that point, she said, "the boy stood up and pointed to . . .
the three classroom 'coaches' huddled around a walkie-talkie.
'Miss,' he said, 'don't listen to them! You be you. Talk to me!
I'm a person! Be a person, Miss. Be you!' " I thought that boy
deserved a prize, instead of a detention.

The training system that the teacher had to undergo, which
is known and marketed as No Nonsense Nurturing, had been
"successfully utilized," according to the group's promotional
materials, in schools "throughout the country." Among the
larger districts that had bought into the program were Mem-
phis, Denver, Charlotte, and Cleveland, and the badly under-
funded schools of Tulsa, Oklahoma, which reportedly paid
some $300,000 for a two-day training session for its teachers.
Similar programs, marketed to school officials under different

brand names, are widely used in other districts elsewhere in the nation.

At a high school in New Haven where almost every child was Black or Latino, teachers were instructed not to let their students ask them questions if there's something they don't understand in the presentation of a lesson. "There Are No Questions" was the rule given to the teachers by the principal, according to a former teacher at the school, who described the "draconian discipline system" and the school's demand for "perfect behavioral compliance." Teachers were told they should not "engage" [*sic*] with a student's question because this might run the risk of ruining the pacing of their lessons.

Highly prescriptive time allocations are important too at these kinds of schools—even for the most routine activities that take place in a classroom, like switching from one lesson to the next one. These tightly timed transitions seem to have been modeled on business-minded practices of speeding up production—in a warehouse or a factory, for instance. About a dozen years ago, a newly founded charter school here in Massachusetts spelled out a detailed script intended to be used by teachers: "Scholars, yesterday you transitioned to Reading in 38 seconds. Your challenge now is to transition in 35 seconds. I am waiting for 100 percent eye contact." Even the simple act of passing in a set of papers had been subjected to a rigid protocol of timing. "Flow them forward," according to the script. "Five seconds, ten seconds, thirteen seconds. Very good. Now flow to the right."

Critics of these practices, as they've been evolving, have tended to focus mostly on high-profile charter schools. But practices like the speed-up regimen have often been adopted in regular, non-charter schools as well. At a public school near the South Loop of Chicago, I watched a group of eight-year-olds sitting in a circle as their teacher counted down the seconds between commands that she was giving. "Four, three, two, one, zero"—clap! clap!—"turn and face your partner." "Four, three, two, one, zero"—clap! clap!— "talk and share." Scarcely fifteen seconds later: "Four, three, two, one, zero"—clap! clap!—"go back to your chairs." While the teacher counted, children were instructed to hold two fingers in the air to signal to the teacher that they were waiting for the next command. If a child failed to lift her fingers or turned to face her partner before the teacher clapped her hands, she might get "an automatic" or another reprimand.

Back in Boston, at a perennially unsuccessful public elementary school in the city's South End area, where ninety percent of the students were Black or Latino, another set of strategies for achieving acquiescence on the part of children depended on the use of simulated money. "Stephanie, you're sitting up correctly. I'm giving you five dollars." "Felicia, I like the way you kept in line when we were transitioning. I'm giving you ten dollars." "Derek, you've been fidgeting. Give me back twenty dollars."

Every child had a "money pouch" in which to keep the dollars he or she was earning. According to a friend of mine who worked there as a teacher aide in a class of fourth grade children, the money could be used to pay for certain privileges. "When we were allowed to have a classroom party, for example, there was an admission fee of five hundred dollars." The ones who didn't have that much in their money pouch had to sit in a detention room while other children in the class "were doing something fun, like having a dance party."

The competition between children to accumulate the money that would win them these rewards led into a situation that, unhappily, might have been expected. Some of the kids who hadn't earned enough, or had forfeited so much that their savings were depleted, began to steal from those who had more money in their pouches.

"Once this started happening," according to the teacher aide, "the teacher figured that the only way to deal with it was to punish the entire class by telling them their earnings had to be returned to her. She said the ones who stole the money had 'bankrupted' them all. This was known as a 'communal learning lesson. . . .'"

Incentivizing children by giving or withholding small

rewards is a fairly common practice—most of us remember this from our years in school. But, in this case, the incentivizing process and withholding of rewards had been carried to a point, as the teacher aide noted, beyond all rationality. As in other schools where interruptions of a lesson are discouraged or forbidden, there were strict constraints on letting children leave a class to go out to the restroom except during transition times. If a child couldn't wait, the teacher aide said, he or she "could buy 'a bathroom right'" by taking twenty dollars from their money pouch. What if the child didn't have enough to buy a bathroom right? In that case, he or she could ask for a loan from another child in the class or from "the classroom bank," as it was called.

Placing a price on a child's right to meet a basic need, turning that right into a privilege that a child has to buy—and the whole idea of monetizing childhood behavior to this extreme degree—according to the teacher aide, would have been unthinkable in the school she had attended as a child in a wealthy suburb of New York. I think it would be anathema as well in most of the white and wealthy districts that I visit to the west and north of Boston.

The extensive body of academic writings that have lent respectability to these and other pieces of the disparate agenda tends to obviate the hard edge of these practices. The authors of these studies tend to stick primarily to self-assured statistical abstractions about "important variables" that are "predictive" of "effectiveness" in reaching certain outcomes. "There is a remarkable similarity between our findings and those reported previously by X and Y in two entirely different samples . . ." There is seldom any mention in these writings of telling teachers not to look too happy or making children beg or borrow dollars when they need to pee.

I was talking about the money pouches and the other methods of incentivizing children at that school in Boston with a first grade teacher whose class I used to visit—I will call her Alessandra—who always had a gift for keeping order in her classroom and winning the cooperation of her students by artfully enticing them to dig into their lessons instead of handing down commandments that "ordered" them to learn according to a state-ordained time-table. An activist for children's rights and civil rights since her years in college, she had a good satiric way of debunking practices that she thought demeaning to young children. She also had a blunt and funny way of poking holes in those familiar hortatory slogans, often posted on a classroom wall, which, she felt, promoted too much competition among children at the expense of one another.

She showed me a poster she had seen, one of several like this that she had been collecting. At the top of the poster were these three words, printed in large letters: "WINNERS" (printed blue) "EXCEED EXPECTATIONS" (printed red). Underneath, there was a picture of a goldfish bowl. Six little fish were swimming around in circles in the bowl. But another, more ambitious fish—the one, she said, who was "apparently exceeding expectations"—had leaped right up out of the bowl. He was the one the class was supposed to emulate. She shook her head. "That's one dead goldfish, I'm afraid. . . ."

One of the other posters she'd collected told the children in a first grade class: "If you can't change it, change how you think about it." Altering the way that children think about an unfair situation was apparently a better way of raising their performance, certainly a less expensive way, than by altering that situation.

She also said she thought it was insulting to good teachers to ask them to recycle this simplistic jargon. She told me about a person that she called "the Efficacy man," who was sent into her building when she was a young teacher. "He had some kind of three-point plan to make us more effective—but he said 'efficacious.' It was all a bunch of bloated language about 'competency' and 'rigor'. We'd heard it all before. . . ."

But, as she noted, the jargon keeps on changing. Every couple of years, it seems, another set of codified expressions takes the place of those with which the experts have grown weary. One of the newer bits of jargon is something known as "SLANTING," or "SLANT behavior" as I've seen it posted on a classroom wall. The letters, as I've learned, stand for "Sit up, Look, Ask and Nod, and Track the teacher with your eyes." There's nothing there that's really new. It's pretty much the same old stuff ("Eyes on me! One, two, three!") but wrapped up in a neater package than before.

"SLANT behavior," according to the teacher aide in Boston who told me of the "money pouches" in which children kept the dollars they were earning, had recently become a term of art in behavioral conditioning. Children at her school who did not "exhibit SLANT behavior" ("exhibit" and "display" are the verbs, she said, that teachers were supposed to use in speaking of behavior) could expect to lose a privilege or face another consequence.

Another term to which she introduced me was something known as "Bubble Hugs," which, despite its warm and friendly sound, turned out to be a less-than-friendly strategy for keeping children mute and stiff when filing in the hallways. Children in the early grades, she said, were being taught to cross their arms and grip their hands around their chest and also fill their cheeks with air so they won't talk by accident. "'Catch a bubble! And be careful not to pop it!'—that's what we're supposed to keep reminding them." If they don't do it right, she said, they're brought back to the classroom and have to line up and start filing again.

The bubble-catching rule, as the teacher aide explained, was seen as a "successful strategy" in "silencing small voices." She said she had heard it also at a Head Start center in Ohio where she'd volunteered before she came to Boston. She described it all—Bubble Hugs and SLANTING—as something like performance art: "performing learning," in her words, instead of simply learning, or, in this case, "performing a behavior."

In an incisive and disturbing book, Linda Nathan, the founder and for many years the guiding spirit of the Boston Arts Academy, deconstructs the stated goals and unstated implications of these practices—all of them, she says, part of the "grit" ethos that has come to be familiar in many schools that serve the children of low income in minority communities. She recounts her observations in an urban school—in which she notes that there were no white children—where she watched a group of second graders filing in the corridor, arms crisscrossed around their chests, looking, she says, "as if they're in straitjackets." She also describes a cafeteria where five different classes were eating lunch, all at the same time and all "in complete silence." The purpose, she was told, was to give the kids a "quiet" and "peaceful" moment in the middle of the day. "But," she says, "it felt anything but peaceful. . . . It seemed more like a prison. . . ."

Proponents of these strategies do not, of course, concede that they're intended to be punitive to children. Instead, they say, the ultimate objective is to reconstruct the way the children look upon themselves. According to this argument, poverty and racial segregation and inadequate resources cannot be accepted as excuses for a child's failure to perform at a high level. If children can be trained to alter their self-image from one that's fixed on failure to one that will empower them with fierce determination to "believe" they can succeed, they will then be better able to achieve the long-term goals they may pursue, or those that we have set for them. Training children to "self-regulate"—"self-regulation" is a favored term—is part of the agenda too. "Growth mindset" is another term that's part of the vernacular. It first acquired currency in education circles about ten years ago and, since that time, has fueled a minor industry of conferences and institutes on mindset alteration.

Once these ideas have been locked in place, it's not easy to dislodge them. But can you really give young children a positive belief in what they can achieve by forcing them to spend their days in silence and to walk along the hallways as if they're in straitjackets? Teaching kids to save themselves—*sauve qui peut*—by swallowing hard, suppressing their uniqueness, "exhibiting grit," and marching ever onward to some kind of minimal salvation, has been too willingly accepted as "the answer," "the solution," to the challenges created by an unjust social order. It's not an answer; it's a socially appeasing adaptation to a seemingly eternal system of unequal education. Change the child, not the system. Any disruptive transformations of the system in itself appear to be beyond consideration.

The silencing of voices that the teacher aide described and her words about "performing a behavior" brought to my mind a conversation I recorded in the spring of 2017 when I was in the troubled schools of Petersburg, Virginia. Petersburg was once a center of slave auctions and the site of slave rebellions, but the city has had a complicated history. After the British were driven out in 1784, a section of the city, known as Pocahontas Island, became the home of families of "free Negroes." The population prospered because of the tobacco trade, and by the mid-1800s, the city had become a major railroad hub, but it was impoverished now and could not borrow badly needed money to improve or fully staff its public schools.

At the Robert E. Lee Elementary School, where ninety-six percent of students were Black or Latino and ninety-nine percent were classified as poor, approximately a quarter of the teachers were short-term subs—some of them "subbing for subs," as the superintendent unhappily observed. Naturally,

I was hoping to get into the classrooms and get to know the children and try to get a first-hand sense of what their days in school were like from their own point of view.

Unfortunately, at the time when I was there, the school was in the midst of testing weeks and, as I was told prior to my visit, "no movement [was] permitted in the building" on days when tests were given. So I was not allowed to go into a classroom until the testing was completed.

Once the tests were over, I was escorted to a class of fourth grade children, which the principal apparently had selected for my visit, and finally had a chance to ask the kids some questions. As I usually do when I have this opportunity, I started out by asking fairly simple, open-ended questions. I asked about the books they had been reading and subjects they were studying. Which of their subjects or other class activities did they like the most, or didn't like so much, or didn't like at all? And, because it was the end of May, I asked them how they thought that they had changed, or how they felt the year had gone for them, since they came into this classroom in September.

I ran into a cold stone wall at first. No one seemed to dare to raise their hand. They seemed afraid to answer me. Finally, a boy in one of the back rows, to whom the teacher pointed, raised his hand quite cautiously. "I'm different now," he told me. "I used to play, but now I work. . . ." The teacher urged him to go on. "I think," he said, "I've made a lot of progress in my decision-making skills. . . ."

At that point, it seemed as if a switch had clicked and other children raised their hands. But every answer that they gave me was the same! No matter how I tried, I couldn't seem to get them off that dime.

"Smart decision-making" had come to be another of those codified expressions that are part of the same package as "meeting expectations" and "exceeding expectations." I'd heard the term at teacher-training seminars and had seen it posted sometimes on a classroom wall. But this was the first time I'd heard a bunch of children recycle this idea, as if it were their own.

Not one of those eight- and nine-year-olds seemed to be able to deviate from script and tell me something, anything, that came directly from themselves. What did they think? What did they feel? If I could have talked with them without their principal and teacher in the room, might they have tossed away the script and opened up a little more?

The teacher made it clear that she was pleased with their response. But the tonelessness and flatness with which they gave that dutiful reply stayed in my mind long after I left Petersburg. I'm sure that there were teachers in the school who were willing to allow, and able to elicit, more authentic words and natural expressions of what was in their children's thoughts, even on a day when they had just been laid low by three hours of exams. Still, in a school and district that were under constant pressure from the state to do whatever it might take to bring about "a turnaround" and show the progress they could make, it couldn't have been easy to counteract the message that trickles down through multiple layers of higher-up officials to get the kids to stick to script if they want to save themselves, since no one else apparently will save them.

The name of the school has since been changed. It's a wonder that is took so long. Robert E. Lee no longer has a place of honor on the front wall of the school. But the shadow of plantation days is still a presence there. In a somber citadel of hypersegregation that was fiscally bankrupt at the time when I was there, the programmed voices and robotic recitations of those children just seemed very sad to me. I wondered if the children in that class had any sense at all of their city's history of fighting against servitude.

3

Learned Helplessness

At the time when I began to teach in the Boston schools all those many years ago, obedience instruction was a high priority. A curriculum guide in character education included several pages of obedience quotations. "Every day, in every way, it is our duty to obey." "He who knows how to obey will know how to command." "The first great law is to obey." "We must do the things we must before the thing we may. / We are unfit for any trust until we can and do obey."

When I cited some of this in *Death at an Early Age*, advocates for children took it as a comical and heavy-handed throwback to an era of the past, reminiscent of satiric passages in the writings of Charles Dickens. Even high officials in the Boston schools seemed to be embarrassed by the thudding rhythms of these exhortations to obedience as "our entire duty," as one quotation put it.

They finally did away with those clunky old quotations. The modern incarnations of obedience instruction, as we've seen, are far less simplistic. The difference now is that it's all more systematic and more ingeniously and carefully developed. It's like a seamless universe. Once you're in it, all its crazy little pieces may appear quite logical.

The training program in which teachers were instructed to

stand in "mountain pose" and not to look too happy in their classrooms was only one of many of such programs. Starting about ten years ago, critics of these practices began to circulate a document that was being widely used in training new recruits, primarily for charter schools. The document, which had been developed by a Boston-based nonprofit called Match Education, was given to enrollees in the training program to spell out their obligations, in the language of the manual, as "The Demanding Teacher." The group has since removed the document from public circulation, but the practices that it prescribes are still in use, not only in the charter schools for which it was designed, and the document is emblematic of a way of thinking about children of low income in minority communities.

According to the manual, the role of The Demanding Teacher calls for "six specific beliefs" and "sixteen specific classroom management moves," each of which is then described in painstaking detail. The first three of the six beliefs are these:

Belief 1: "I am the ultimate authority in my classroom."
Belief 2: "My goal in classroom management must be 100%."
Belief 3: "My Patrolling Effort and Behavior Oblongata . . . needs to be strengthened to the point of automaticity. . . ."

Whatever the oblongata, a portion of the brain, has to do with classroom management is not clear at first (that part is developed later in an illustration of the brain), but the numbers somehow make it all sound rational and vaguely scientific.

The "sixteen classroom management moves" begin with fairly ordinary things ("Greet students at the door . . . Circulate . . . [Use] proximity . . .") but then become more serious: "Narrate compliance . . . ," "Stop and stare . . . ," "Dismissal from class . . . ," "Do it again. . . ."

There are also "Three Rules of Authoritative Presence" that teachers are instructed to observe in the presence of their students. Rule 1: "Your body language: Straight, squared up . . ." Rule 2: "How your voice sounds: Loud, decisive, urgent . . . , emotionally neutral." Rule 3: "The words you choose: Formal and concise." Body language and tone of voice are then broken down into five sub-units each, with pictures of a teacher squaring up and standing straight and another who is "droopy," "meek," and "insecure." Teachers are informed that authoritative presence, "contrary to its reputation," is not an inherent quality, but "a skill" one can acquire. A teacher who came into the program and did not have "an overwhelming personality" was able, we are told, to compensate for this by practicing "her presence and her management moves relentlessly."

The picture of the brain that accompanies the reference to "Patrolling Effort" and "Behavior Oblongata" also identifies other sections of the brain, one of which the manual calls

the "Performance Cortex" and another the "Navigational
Lobe." "We discovered three regions of the Teacher Brain that
account for the vast majority of the decisions that teachers
make when they're delivering instruction. . . . The Cortex has
a big part in determining how well you plan and execute your
lessons. . . ."

The manual also verges into language that belongs to eco-
nomics. Time subtracted from instruction by a child's misbehavior is called a "Misbehavior Tax," which must be deducted
from the class's "Effort" rating. It isn't clear if teachers are
intended to do this on some kind of chart that would mean
something to children.

Beyond the strange allusions—the students' Effort ratings,
and the rest—there is the peculiar emphasis on assigning
numbers to all these lists of strategies and possible behaviors.
At some schools, numbers are assigned to different modes of
conversation that children are permitted or forbidden in different situations at different moments of the day. At lunch-
time at one such school, for instance, according to a schedule
for the day, "scholars are silent for the first five minutes" to
"focus" on their meals. At the end of five minutes, the teacher
tells the students, "Good afternoon . . . , scholars. Because of
the Excellence you have demonstrated in your behavior . . . ,
you have earned Level Two Talk." What is Level Two Talk?
How many other levels are included in the list? It turns out

there are six in all. Level Zero is described as "a silent level," which children must observe when the teacher's talking to the class. Level One is whispering. Level Two is group talk. Level Three is for "whole class conversation." Level Four is "presentation voice." Level Five is "out of control" and always forbidden.

Six beliefs. Three rules. Sixteen moves. Five levels of conversation, plus Level Zero: silence. . . . To people in the ordinary world, it all might sound like some kind of industrious neurosis, a clinical condition in which unhealthy people make long exhausting lists to try to organize and govern their anxieties about the things—or, in this case, the children—they fear they can't control.

On an autumn day in Boston, not quite seven years ago, I was at an elementary school in Dorchester, not far from the neighborhood where I had started teaching. A number of the strategies developed for the training of The Demanding Teacher had been adopted or adapted slightly for use within this school, where almost every child in the classrooms that I visited was Black or Latino. But when a child proved to be resistant to these methods of control, the school had a stronger medicine in store.

There was a closet in the hallway of the school where children who committed certain misbehaviors were placed in isolation, sometimes for extended periods of time. The door to the closet would be locked, but there was a window in the door through which a child was supposed to be observed. The closet was described as "the Calm-down room," which was apparently intended to make it sound like something therapeutic.

Locking kids in closets, where they often wet themselves, or defecate, and cry out for their mothers, turned out to be a more familiar practice than I knew. In one instance in New York, according to the New York Daily News, "a tiny padded room . . . about the size of a walk-in closet" became "a real-life nightmare for two young boys," one in the first grade, the other in kindergarten. The kindergarten child, according to his mother, underwent an anxiety attack and had to be taken to the hospital.

As I've since discovered, there are thirty-one states in which this practice is legally allowed—or else permitted by loopholes in the law. In more than half those states, including Massachusetts and New York, children may be placed in lockdown rooms even when they pose no threat or danger to themselves or others. According to a national watchdog group called Solitary Watch, children of color are far more likely than white children to be placed in isolation rooms. In the District of Columbia, in the 2015–16 academic year, ninety-four percent of the children placed in "restraint or seclusion" were African

American, and the other six percent were Native American, mixed race, or Latino.

"Calm-down rooms" is only one of the soothingly misleading terms I've heard to designate these places of restraint. They're sometimes called "Reflection Rooms" or "Quiet Rooms" or "Relaxation Rooms," although the children who are crying for their mothers are obviously neither quiet nor "relaxing." The use of this Orwellian language cannot disguise the cruelty of treating kids of any age or any race this way.

But when it comes to physical abuse, placing kids in lockdown rooms is not the worst of miseries they may undergo. In a number of states, physical beatings of children as young as six years old are also an accepted practice in too many of their schools. Corporal punishment is officially prohibited in almost all the Northern states, but it's still allowed in Arkansas, Texas, Mississippi, Alabama, Florida, and other Southern states, as well as Indiana, Colorado, Arizona, Idaho, Missouri, Wyoming, and Kentucky. In all, it's allowed in twenty-three states and, where it's allowed, the racial disproportions are evident again. Black boys are almost twice as likely as white boys—and Black girls three times as likely as white girls—to be given corporal punishment.

There's nothing therapeutic about the stated purpose of these practices. The Texas Education Code, for instance, defines the use of corporal punishment as "the deliberate infliction of physical pain by hitting, paddling, spanking, slapping, or any other physical force used as a means of discipline." According to Elizabeth Gershoff, a professor of human development at the University of Texas, "evidence from other states" confirms that practices like these are used to punish children for forms of misbehavior that could hardly be considered serious or dangerous. Children, she notes, have frequently been beaten for "being late to class," "violating dress code," "sleeping in class," "going to the bathroom without permission"—even for "mispronouncing words" or "laughing in the hallways."

Wooden paddles are the standard instruments of discipline. The dimensions of the paddles are specified in detail—two feet long, three inches wide in one Alabama district, for example. Other guidelines indicate how many blows may be inflicted on a child, depending on a child's age or grade, whether there must be a witness present, and whether parents must be notified or give prior consent. These rules, as many press accounts and legal suits have documented through the years, are not consistently observed, but even when they're followed to the letter, the entire protocol of detailed stipulations about the proper methods and conditions for inflicting pain on children in a public school has a note of the macabre.

Approximately 70,000 children were beaten in their public schools or charter schools in 2017–18, the most recent year for which numbers are available, according to the U.S. Department of Education Civil Rights Data Collection and the New York–based Hechinger Report. But this and other estimates are drawn from the numbers reported by the schools in which these practices are used, and the reliability of these reports is sometimes held in question. Then, too, even where the consent of a child's parent is required prior to a beating, consent is all too easily coerced when parents are advised that non-consent may lead to other punishments, such as suspensions from the school, which often prove to be a prelude to expulsion.

Attempts to prohibit corporal punishment by recourse to the federal courts have historically proven unsuccessful. The U.S. Supreme Court has refused to intervene in cases in which parents sought relief in the wake of beatings given to their children. A Supreme Court ruling in 1977 in a Florida case, *Ingraham v. Wright*, held that corporal punishment of students in a public school is not prohibited by the cruel and unusual punishment clause of the Eighth Amendment, although the ruling noted that the same clause in the Eighth Amendment does (at least in theory, if not in actual practice) prohibit corporal punishment of inmates in a prison. The five-to-four decision in the *Ingraham* case was written by Justice Lewis Powell, who had been appointed to the court by Richard Nixon six years earlier.

Three decades later, in a case in Texas in 2008, in which

an eighteen-year-old student had been severely beaten with a wooden paddle in her school in San Antonio, the court declined the opportunity to overrule the earlier decision. According to Yale law professor Justin Driver in his book *The Schoolhouse Gate*, the student in the Texas case had left her school before the start of classes to buy herself "a breakfast taco" at a store across the street. "Soon thereafter," she was called into the office of the acting principal, who told her she had broken a "closed-campus" regulation. She was ordered to "bend over . . . with her buttocks raised" in order to be beaten. When she refused, she was restrained by "two other school officials" and received her beating with a four-foot paddle, which left her with "her buttocks bleeding" and a swollen hand, which was injured when she used it in an effort to defend herself. Her mother picked her up from school "and took her directly to the hospital."

Other incidents like this, which involve much younger children, continue to surface in videos and local media accounts. A five-year-old Black child in a kindergarten class in a school in Texas in 2016 was beaten with a paddle because he stuck his tongue out at a teacher. In another case, a six-year-old Black child at a school in Florida in 2021 was dragged out of his kindergarten class by a school official who wrapped his arm around his throat and then, according to a local television station, the child was "pushed down into a chair and choked."

In yet another case, which was the subject of a long and detailed article by Rebecca Klein in the Huffington Post in 2018, a Black girl in an eighth grade class in Holmes County, Mississippi, was accused of having left her coat in a teacher's classroom and, when she said that it was not her coat and began to walk away, "the man came up from behind her . . . and put her in a choke hold."

The "physical punishment of Black bodies. . . ," according to Aaron Kupchik, a professor of sociology and criminal justice at the University of Delaware, "doesn't arise out of nowhere. There is a historical trajectory." The states and counties where lynchings were most common are those in which Black and Latino children are most likely to experience these physical transgressions at the hands of school officials. The use of corporal punishment, at least as the term is generally defined—by beating a child with a wooden paddle—is believed to have declined in the course of recent years, but this and other instances of placing hands on children—lifting a child from a chair by the child's collar, slamming a child against a wall in a fit of adult fury—continue to be often-unreported vestiges of an old benighted order.

At the far end of the spectrum of racialized abuse, children of color are also far more likely than white children to be arrested in their schools, at the behest of school officials, and given a stay in juvenile detention of one form or other. Some of these incidents have been given media attention when they were caught on body cameras if police were wearing them.

In September of 2019, for example, a little girl named Kaia, six years old, was arrested at a charter school in Florida because she had "a tantrum" in her classroom and allegedly had kicked a school official. According to the Orlando Sentinel, the child had recovered from her tantrum by the time the officer came into the office at the school, where someone on the staff was reading a story to her, which had helped her to calm down. "Don't put handcuffs on," the child pleaded, but the person who was reading the story to her did not intervene as the officer detained her.

The child was placed in zip ties and literally dragged out of the building and placed in a police car and brought to a juvenile center, where she was fingerprinted and received a mug shot. (The child was so small that she had to be placed on a step stool for the mug shot to be taken.) Charges against the child were ultimately dropped, but, for many months, according to her grandmother, she was having nightmares and reverted to bed-wetting. Almost two years after the event, the child's grandmother said, Kaia was still in therapy to bring her "out of [her] despair."

Another Black child at the school, a little boy, also six years old, had been handed over to police on the same day that

Kaia was arrested. It wasn't clear how frequently other children at this school or other schools in Florida had been subjected to this punishment. A bill has since been enacted in Florida to prohibit the arrest of children who are six years old or younger. For children seven years old and older, no such protection is afforded by the law. In twenty-five other states, there is no minimum age at which a child may be subject to arrest or prosecution.

In one of the most egregious cases, this one in Tennessee in a county close to Nashville, the mass arrests of eleven Black children, four of whom were girls, after an altercation at a playground, led to an investigation which revealed that as many as 1,500 children had been illegally arrested in the county since 2006. The juvenile judge who oversaw this series of arrests also ran the juvenile jail in which these children were detained. A white woman and political conservative who also had a popular radio talk show on a local station, the judge later said that she was "proud of what this court has accomplished" and how it has "positively affected" children's lives.

The willingness of any school to hand its students over to police, instead of providing counselors to help them when they lose their self-control, is troubling enough, no matter what the child's race or age. Treating a child who commits no grievous sins as a precocious criminal is abhorrent in itself. And, as in the case of lockdown rooms and other forms of physical abuse, the racial differentials have again been clearly documented. Black girls, according to a study of "School Discipline by Race and Gender," published by the Georgetown Law Center on Poverty and Inequality in 2020, are 3.6 times more likely than white girls to be arrested at their schools. They are also seven times more likely to be given multiple suspensions from those schools. This, too, has its roots in history. Young Black girls have long been seen, not only by officials in their schools, as more suspicious, less to be trusted, than white girls of their age.

The story of little Kaia, dragged from her school in Florida because she had "a tantrum," captured more than usual attention from the media, in part because she was so small and her purported crime so trivial. The white policeman who hauled her off later boasted to a friend how many other children he'd detained. This, too, was caught on video.

4

Ironies and Desolation

There is an elementary and middle school in Boston's Black community that bears the name of Dr. Martin Luther King Jr. It's an old and tired-looking structure, built in 1937 and originally named for a former school official. In 1965, Dr. King stood on the front steps of the building and spoke through a megaphone to a crowd of parents and religious figures who were leading the charge in the integration struggle. Three years later, after his assassination in April 1968, the school was renamed in his honor.

But ironies abound. The school today, sad to say, is one more vivid and heartbreaking case of hopes and dreams abandoned and betrayed. In a building that held about 500 students, as the principal told me when I visited the school most recently, in 2019, "I think I may have twelve white children." In academic terms, the school was rated in the bottom ten percent among a total of about 1,800 public elementary and secondary schools in all of Massachusetts.

It's not a physically inviting place for kids to spend their days. There were ugly water holes in the ceiling of the first of several classrooms that I visited, and peeling paint in the gloomy metal stairways. I sat in on an eighth grade science class that took place in an ancient-looking lab that had no lab equipment. It was a long and narrow room in which the rows of science tables took up so much space that the students in a back row, beside whom I was sitting, could barely hear the teacher and couldn't see what he had written on the white board he was using. One of the students, a tall Black girl who was toying with her cell phone, turned to me with a friendly but sardonic smile. She shrugged her shoulders, with her hands spread out, as if to say, "This is what we're used to."

According to the website of the Boston Public Schools, "The Martin Luther King Jr. K–8 School exemplifies the true meaning of Dr. King's dream." I had to wonder if the writer of that statement had spent much time in classes there and actually believed this.

The principal was a kind and likable person and had no hesitation about allowing me to visit in classrooms of my choosing. But it seemed that officials at the school department had some qualms about my visit. They sent a person from the central office to oversee my conversation with the principal.

The poor academic rating of the school came as no surprise to me. The numbers were well known. It was the sense of physical decay in a building meant to honor the memory of Dr. King that lingered in my memory. Other schools in Boston were not only tired-looking but in far worse disrepair. Squalid bathrooms—sinks with broken faucets and no hot water, toilets that could not be flushed, and toilet stalls that had no doors—were a common problem. At one of the schools in a neighborhood where I lived when I was teaching, an eleven-year-old student told a reporter from The Boston Globe that she avoided going to the bathrooms because they were so vile. She had taught herself a kind of game that she called "the pee dance"—rocking back and forth, according to The Globe, and lifting up one leg and shaking it—in order to distract herself when she had to urinate. One day, she said, it didn't work. She had to ask permission "to go to the nurse's office for a change of clothes."

Stinky and disgusting bathrooms are the kinds of ugly details that tell the children in these schools how little their sense of self-respect is valued. Sometimes when I'm visiting a school, if I need a restroom break, I'll tell the school official who's escorting me that I'll just use a restroom that we're passing in the hall. "Oh no!" I'm told. "You don't want to go in there. We have a nicer bathroom in the office for our visitors. . . ." If the bathroom we were passing would offend a grown-up visitor, why would it not be offensive to a child?

Teachers in other cities tell me of these and other incivilities in the schools in which they work. A number of these schools have no functional cooling systems and sometimes have to send their students home on very hot and humid days. In some of the same districts where construction and repair have been deferred for decades, the heating systems have broken down in the cold of winter. In Baltimore, according to a CBS News report, "teachers posted photos of children bundled up in freezing rooms," wearing coats and gloves, when the boiler systems failed. "It's unbearable. There are icicles in the classroom. The cold water jug is frozen. . . . It's inhumane. . . ," the mother of one of the children said.

In Lee County, Virginia, in the southwest corner of the state, a teacher said she had to rearrange the children's desks from one day to the next because of water spilling from the ceiling. "Some days, it's a trickle," according to a newspaper in Roanoke. Other days, the teacher said, "it's like a waterfall coming down." At least, in these extreme and shocking cases, press accounts can sometimes stir sufficient outrage to compel officials in a state to come up with money for emergency repairs. But the pervasive dreariness, the low-level indignities, the gloomy-looking corridors, the schools where kids are herded down to have their lunch in unattractive, often airless basement cafeterias—none of this is stark enough, or sufficiently unusual, to awaken any sense of urgency.

According to a Washington Post story in 2018, public schools in the United States were forty-five years old on average, and in the old industrial cities, usually much older. "The last time Congress debated school infrastructure spending was in 2009," when school construction funds were initially included in President Obama's "stimulus deal." But the line item was subtracted from the deal when the president found himself unable to win even minimal Republican support. The infrastructure bill passed by Congress in November 2021 did not include funding for school construction and repair. And the ill-fated Build Back Better bill, although it did originally include funding to build new schools and modernize old ones, was finally taken off the table, as advocates for children unhappily recall, when congressional conservatives rejected it. By the fall of 2022, the average age of a public school had risen to nearly fifty years.

At state and local levels, when federal help is not forthcoming, policy-makers and political officials wring their hands and claim that local funds to meet these needs are simply not available. Some of them also have a practiced way of fending off the protests of poor parents by questioning whether school repair or disrepair will actually make much difference in the performance of a child. "Sure, it would be great," they say, "if we could give those schools a fresh new coat of paint, fix up the children's bathrooms, put in a new heating system, or give the students in this school or that school a nicer place to have their lunch. But none of this has any real connection with the children's motivation or their academic gains. . . ."

If this were true, if physical conditions had no impact on a child's motivation and eagerness for learning, we'd need to ask why all those very costly and exclusive private prep schools up here in New England, for example, to which successive generations of the orchestrating classes tend to send their children in the secondary years, take so much pride in showing applicants and visitors their handsome and historic redbrick Georgian buildings with carefully trimmed ivy, and new, impressive, glass-walled student centers, designed sometimes by a well-known architect, and, at some of these schools, galleries for students' art or priceless art collections.

Why spend all this money? Why badger their alumni for donations to replace an old but decent dining hall or library, or put up a new science center built around a courtyard where kids can get together between classes and work with one another on an art or science project? Why bother about keeping up a lovely stretch of landscaped lawn along a winding road that leads to the main buildings? We know the answer to these questions without asking. Beautiful environments quietly convey a sense of dignity to children. Squalor and decrepitude soil their mentalities.

Many of the older schools I've been describing are not merely unattractive and demoralizing places with serious heat and cooling problems. An alarming number of these buildings are also plagued with lead-based paint that crumbles from the walls and ceilings.

The injury to cerebral performance that children undergo

from breathing or chewing flakes or chips of lead-based paint is often irreversible. As long as fifty years ago, pediatricians and neurologists warned us of these dangers to a child's cognitive capacities. But, in spite of their warnings and the compelling medical literature that delineates those dangers, lead infestation continues unabated in all too many schools.

A study of environmental hazards in the District of Columbia, released by the National Academy of Medicine in 2017, examined the extent of lead paint exposure and its effects on children in the district and similarly endangered children elsewhere in the nation. The study noted that federal legislation enacted in 2008 "made the presence of lead-based paint . . . illegal in all residential dwellings . . . and in child-occupied facilities . . . , built before 1978." (The average public school, as we have seen, was built before that date.) But enforcement of the law, as parents seldom learn until it's far too late, has too often been impeded or resisted at state and local levels; and, despite the law, no federal regulations compel the states to test for lead in public schools and, if it's present at high levels, to get rid of it entirely. In 2014, six years after the toothless federal legislation of 2008, according to the nonprofit Lead Safe America Foundation, lead hazards in the public schools still were "pretty universal," at least in older neighborhoods in the fifty cities that the group surveyed.

In those older neighborhoods there is also a high likelihood that the deteriorated housing in which children live contains the same lead hazards. The combined effect of both these factors—unsafe schools, unsafe housing—has historically taken its highest toll on young children of color, according to the CDC and other governmental or independent sources. "Most of the families at risk for lead poisoning each year," as the national health organization Healthline noted in 2022, "are Black families." "An increased prevalence of lead poisoning in Black communities, especially in Black children, is an unequivocal example of environmental racism," as Healthline puts the matter bluntly.

The dangers, moreover, are present not only in the air that children breathe or in chips of lead they chew. In many districts, children cannot drink the water from the fountains in their schools because of lead and other toxins, either in the water sources or, more often, in archaic lead and copper piping in the plumbing system of the school. In some cities where inspections have been cursory or incomplete or never carried out at all, high lead levels in the paint or water have not been detected until a child or a group of children became sick enough to end up in a hospital.

In a powerful series titled "Toxic City," The Philadelphia Inquirer described a scenario of "filthy schools and unsafe conditions," "acres of flaking and peeling paint likely containing lead," and "dangerously high levels of cancer-causing

asbestos fibers" from "crumbling pipe insulation," deteriorated ceilings, and broken tiles in the floor. Often, said the
paper, the district knows about these perils "but downplays
them to [children's] parents." At one elementary school where
"paint chips fluttered from the ceiling of a first grade classroom" and landed on a child's desk, the six-year-old, who was
afraid to get up from his chair and throw the paint chips in
the trash, according to the paper, "put them in his mouth
[and] swallowed them."

It wasn't long before the effects on his behavior became
obvious. His teacher started to assign him to the "red zone"
because he was talking out of turn or became too restless to
stay still in his chair. Within a month, his parents said that he
was having "mood swings. Frequent stomachaches. Inability
to finish sentences. Overwhelming sadness." Within another
month, he was in the hospital. "The level of lead in [his]
blood," according to the paper, "was . . . nine times higher
than the level at which doctors worry about permanent damage to the brain. . . ." Even then, The Inquirer notes, it was
another seven months before the city got around to sending
in a crew to cover up the lead-based paint that poisoned him.

Toxins in the walls. Toxins in the air. Toxins in the water.
In Newark, New Jersey, in 2016, according to The New York
Times, "high lead levels were found in the drinking water in
more than half the city's . . . schools." Some of the schools

had to shut down the drinking fountains. Thousands of children needed to be tested in order to determine whether, or how much, they had been damaged.

In the same year, parents at two schools in Boston were alerted to the risks their children had been facing because of high lead levels in the water they'd been drinking from the hallway fountains. The parents were advised that it was up to them to arrange to put their children through a lengthy protocol of testing. In other states and districts that lack the will or lack the funds to replace the lead and copper plumbing, signs are sometimes posted over water faucets warning children not to drink from them. "If you're thirsty," said one high school student in New York where a warning sign was posted on a faucet, "you don't think about it—you just drink it. . . ."

A friend of mine, a part-time instructor at a college in New York, whose son had attended an elementary school where lead paint was detected, told me that, when he took him to be tested, the boy was diagnosed with damage to his learning capability. The child had had no problems of this nature when he was in preschool but, by the time he was in second grade, he began to find it hard to focus on his lessons. Like the boy in Philadelphia who had swallowed chips of lead that had landed on his desk, he became a problem for his teachers. He was placed in a program for children with "behavioral delays." He never totally recovered and failed to finish high school.

"No one in the system *did* this to my son," he said. They just left him there to suffer for their negligence or apparent lack of funds. His father described this as a kind of "slow-motion process" of institutional destruction. He called it "passive genocide," since nobody had wished this on his child. It was just, he said, "the way things were" in the dilatory workings of the system, although he believed that officials in the district must have known about these dangers that their students were incurring. . . .

When state and city leaders tell parents in poor neighborhoods that they empathize with their concerns about the presence of toxins and other dangers in their children's schools but say they cannot act on those concerns for now, they typically claim that their hands are tied, as we have seen, because of fiscal shortages. And sometimes, in the wake of a genuine fiscal crisis, this is obviously true. When the local economy goes into a sudden steep decline, cities are forced to put off renovations for a period of time and also cut back routine funding for their schools. When the economy recovers, parents are told, the needed funds will be restored.

It doesn't always work that way, however. All too often once these cuts—"austerity budgets," as they're called—are put in place, they remain in place long after any point at which they can be reasonably justified. In the 1970s, for example, there was a major national recession. In New York City, an emergency plan was put into effect, which called for steep reductions in funding for the schools. But as late as 1999, when the economy was booming and millionaires and billionaires were being celebrated in the social pages of the local press, I was walking into public schools in some of the poorest sections of the Bronx that were every bit as desolate as they'd been when I first described those schools in *Savage Inequalities* almost ten years before.

There was no shortage of money in New York City at this time. These were the years when trendy clubs and restaurants and new boutique hotels and elegant stores with famous names were thriving in Manhattan. Developers like Donald Trump were erecting glitzy tributes to themselves and to their newfound wealth, while children I was meeting in wretched-looking schools were being left to pay the price for the myth of scarcity.

The same pattern repeats itself in other states and cities as economic crises come and go. In the wake of the recession of 2008, funding for construction and repair of public schools was often cut back once again. But, over the course of the next ten years, those cutbacks in too many states were only partially and grudgingly restored and, in many districts, were not restored at all. When Covid struck in 2020, the prolonged postponement of construction and repair—and the lack of functional ventilation in so many of the oldest schools—added to the crisis faced by the cities as they struggled to make buildings safe enough for children to return.

Here in Boston, where more than half the city's schools were built eighty or more years ago, the last significant school construction took place in the 1960s and 1970s, when dozens of new schools had been built. In 2013, when an earnest-seeming mayor-to-be, Marty Walsh, was running for election, he made a campaign pledge to allocate $1 billion for major renovation and construction. Four years later, his promise unfulfilled, he made the pledge again. As often happens in these cases of foot-dragging, he appointed a commission to look into the matter and come up with a proposal for a plan of action. The proposal, when it was finally released, allowed the city ten more years for renovation or construction of a dozen schools, which would, of course, bring no benefit to any of those children who came into their kindergarten year when he began to make these promises.

"By any measure, the Boston schools should be flush with cash," according to a Boston Globe report in 2019, because the economy in Boston had been booming. But, "for all the city's wealth," the paper said, students in the district were still attending school in "decades-old buildings" plagued by leaking ceilings and shortages of children's basic needs.

Since that time, more ambitious promises have been made.

In the spring of 2022, the newly elected mayor of Boston, Michelle Wu, announced a proposal to speed up school construction and repair. Some of this work has now been done. More is on the planning boards for the years to come. It's hard to know how much longer it will be before the children in every Boston neighborhood are provided with a school that does not endanger their well-being or offend their dignity.

When I visit with children in their classrooms in other urban districts where buildings have long been left in ugly disrepair, I have sometimes been startled by their clear perception of what they've been denied. "You have Clean Things. We do not have," a third grade student in the South Bronx told me in a letter that her teacher sent me. I later met this little girl when I visited her classroom. She was only eight years old, but she already had a vivid sense of the meaning of inequity.

5

Models of the Possible

Ever since the year in which I taught in Boston and the subsequent years in which I worked with parents here and in other urban centers in the early stages of the drive for integration, school officials in many of those chronically troubled and unsuccessful districts have been telling us our efforts were misguided and unneeded and, as they've argued, might do more harm than good. Instead, they would tell us—we have heard this countless times—of a new reform they were about to put in place that would solve the problems they were facing in the system as it stands. The new reform in question, we would typically be told, had "worked" in cities X and Y, "so we're going to implement it here."

It's going to take a mighty plow to clear away those multiple cycles of reform that claim to have made separate schools more equal, each of which has had its hour in the sun, been dutifully adopted, briefly praised in media accounts, and then abandoned when children made no gains.

In Boston, in the 1960s, there was a program with the upbeat but misleading name of "Operation Counterpoise," one of the earliest but clumsiest attempts to introduce Black children to a disparate agenda. The program, according to the Boston School Committee, was intended to compensate

Black children for the tiringly and insultingly repeated cultural "disadvantages" of their families. The committee baldly stated that "Operation Counterpoise" would not be needed in the city's white communities, where familial values were supposedly not lacking and family structure was allegedly intact. In reality, the program offered nothing more than a culturally ignorant cover-up for a system that was racist to its core.

Other reforms that came and went were less insulting to Black children and their parents, but seldom made a noticeable difference in the course of time. One of the heavily promoted models of reform was the movement called "Effective Schools." (My teacher friend Alessandra, as we've seen, spoke about "the Efficacy man" who, she said, was brought into her school and had some kind of three-point plan "to make us 'more effective.'" She also said, "He spoke to us in bullying tones" and, when she asked a practical question, rudely shut her down.)

Along with the movement for Effective Schools, there were also "Exemplary Schools," "Renaissance Schools," "Quality Schools" (there was also a program known as "Schools of Total Quality," a term that was borrowed from the world of business management), and schools that were divided into smaller units, each of them rebranded an "Academy," as if they were small prep schools in New England. Some of these smaller schools, when they had a gifted principal, seemed to make a degree of progress for a time. But, when the principal decided to move on, the gains that he or she had made would almost always disappear.

There were also a number of programs that touted potent-sounding terms like "Mastery" and "High Potential." "All children in this school can learn to their potential" if we just get tough on them—the early seeds of the "No Excuses" era. A schoolhouse bully named Joe Clark, the principal of East-side High in Paterson, New Jersey, walked the hallways of the school with a baseball bat and bullhorn and expelled or suspended students who did not conform to his code of discipline. He was treated with adulation by much of the media and by white conservatives in Washington—he also became the subject of a movie—until he resigned to enjoy his stardom on the lecture circuit before he became director of a house of youth detention. When I visited the school after his retirement, teachers told me of the social wreckage he had left behind.

All of this was prelude to the full-blown reification of the disparate agenda as it's been evolving in the decades since. It didn't work. The gap between the races has not narrowed and, as the insightful and meticulous Nikole Hannah-Jones and older researchers of my generation have documented clearly, the gap has only widened since the drive for racial integration was stopped in its tracks by the early 1990s. But the addiction to these cycles of spurious reform, right up to the cult of altering the mindset of a child within the unaltered borders of a segregated system, has been a continuing force in keeping an unjust status quo intact.

Another major obstacle to integration efforts is, of course, the charter school phenomenon. Advocates for fair and equal public education have consumed a vast amount of energy in trying to slow down the expansion of this movement. But corporate groups and right-leaning millionaires and billionaires have been pouring money into many of the states to carry out promotional campaigns to raise the caps on charter schools, and business-minded leaders of both parties in those states have often joined the chorus of support for private competition in meeting public needs.

Charter schools have tended to be unembarrassed bastions of racial segregation at its most extreme and powerful generating centers for the harshest versions of the disparate agenda. In the long run, however, if there were no charter schools or if the pace of their expansion could be brought under control, we would still be living with a dual system that betrays and eviscerates the legacy of *Brown*. And even if the charter schools were not extracting badly needed funds from the public schools with which they've been competing, the myth of scarcity would still be there, the weary-looking and aesthetically repellent buildings and the ever-present risks of toxins in the water and the air.

Some of the best-known charter chains do, admittedly, appear to be successful in raising the level of their average scores, in part by unconceded selectivity in the children they enroll, and it's easily understandable that Black and Latino parents who see no other options are frequently attracted to these schools by their great finesse in marketing what they claim to have achieved. But most, for all their promotional skills, have not delivered on these claims. Privatized Jim Crow education cannot close up the nation's wounds.

In her powerful essays and public presentations, Nikole Hannah-Jones has brought us back to the heart of the issue I have been addressing here. In an interview with the public radio program This American Life in 2015, she drew upon the many visits she had made to segregated schools and recounted the words of school officials who would tell her of programs they had put in place or would soon be introducing. " 'We are going to really focus on literacy. We are going to start an early college high school . . . We're going to improve teacher quality. We're going to replace the principal.'" And, she said, they would speak about "more testing. . . ."

"They're always talking really about the same things," she went on. And those things, she said, are the things we know "aren't working." There was only "one thing that really worked," she argued, "and cut the achievement gap between Black and white students by half." An interviewer asked her what she meant.

"Integration," she replied.

She has also written and spoken of her own experience as a little girl in Iowa who rode the bus every day, "starting in second grade and all the way through high school," in order to go to school in an "almost entirely white and very wealthy" neighborhood, in a voluntary program which, she says, was "transformative" for her. And she has written of similar programs—some of which were voluntary, others ordered by the courts—that allowed Black children to cross the borders between neighborhoods or districts in order to attend better schools with a better funding base than those in their communities.

But many of those programs, as she notes, have since been curtailed, or cut off entirely, in the face of opposition from local politicians. A voluntary inter-district program between St. Louis and a number of its suburbs, which had begun in 1981, was virulently opposed by Missouri's Attorney General, John Ashcroft, who later served as U.S. Attorney General in the George W. Bush administration. The program, which I observed in 1985 in two of the suburbs where it was initially adopted, relies upon state funding for transportation and other costs, and was continually faced with threats of cancellation. After a series of short-term extensions, it is now scheduled to be terminated in 2024.

A somewhat similar program of cross-district integration, which began in Milwaukee in the 1970s and, at its peak in the early 1990s, served as many as 7,000 children, was terminated by Wisconsin governor Scott Walker in 2015. According to Bob Peterson, who served on the Milwaukee School Board from 2019 to 2023 and was a founding editor of Rethinking Schools, Walker's role in ending the program was applauded by conservatives and local voucher advocates.

Other programs, however, have survived and, for all the political obstacles and legal challenges they often face, are still flourishing today. One of the longest-lasting of these programs, and presently the largest, which began here in the metro Boston area in 1966, continues to serve about 3,100 children of color, who ride the bus each day from Roxbury and Dorchester and other Boston neighborhoods to more than thirty suburbs, some of them contiguous with, or very close to, Boston, others as much as an hour's ride away. I was involved with this program from the start. Several of the mothers of children I was teaching at the school in Dorchester where I'd been working just one year before were among the strong, determined leaders who conceived and organized the struggle that it took to bring this to fruition.

The program began after a group of parents in Dorchester and Roxbury started to bus their children, at their own expense, to an elementary school on Boston's wealthy Beacon Hill that had space available, and then to schools in other Boston neighborhoods. This early effort, which was known as Operation Exodus, was founded by an education activist and mother of five children by the name of Ellen Jackson, whom I used to visit at the storefront office where she worked on Blue Hill Avenue in Roxbury.

But the lack of public funding to pay for transportation and the hostile racial climate in the city as a whole quickly led the parents to shift the focus of their struggle in a new direction. They looked outward at the suburbs, where school officials in a few progressive districts—Newton was one, Brookline was another—joined forces with the parents in developing the first stage of the program, which is known as Metco.

The program, which children usually enter in the first few years of school, has a four-year high school graduation rate of approximately ninety-five percent. It's always had its critics, but not among the many thousand families whose kids have been on waiting lists to get into the program and not among the friends and teachers, like myself (I taught in the program in its first two years), who have seen its students go on to higher education and then into professional careers or leadership positions in the business world. Others became teachers, sometimes in the districts they'd attended.

My longtime friend and close collaborator, Julia Walker, who is now ninety-one years old, was one of the original parents who seized the opportunity to enroll their children in the program. Her oldest son rode the bus to Brookline, where he made friends easily and quickly. After college, where he studied musicology, he returned to the Brookline schools and worked there as a teacher for more than thirty years. A teacher of music in the elementary grades (he was a gifted jazz and blues guitarist), he wedded the blues and folkloric music into racial history, tracing the path of jazz and the blues along the line of Black migration northward to Chicago. I watched him once performing for the children, who sat around him on the floor—white, Latino, Black, and Asian—singing along and holding hands with one another.

Others in Julia's family have taken the same journey. Her great-granddaughter, whom I will call Emily, rides the bus from Roxbury each morning to a school in suburban Belmont, where she's thriving academically. The child told me a couple of years ago that the mother of her closest friend did not invite her to her daughter's birthday party, but the daughter told her mother that she didn't want a party if her friend was not invited. The daughter won the battle. (The mother ended up driving into Boston to bring Emily to the party.) Emily is in high school now. She and her friends from Belmont High sometimes have pajama parties in one another's homes on holidays or weekends.

It isn't always peace and joy for children in the program. Racist words and other signs of ignorance and bigotry are sometimes heard. But teachers and mentors and district-wide coordinators have been trained to intervene when these incidents occur, and carefully tailored anti-racist workshops are increasingly required in participating districts. Inevitably, in the secondary years, there are frequently those famous "separate tables"—self-segregation on the part of kids of color—which are often seized upon by critics of the program as if that very natural behavior of clustering together (I did the same with my Jewish classmates when I was at Harvard) was some kind of damning proof that "the whole thing is a failure."

I have mentioned that I taught in Metco for two years. My teaching stint in Boston had ended prematurely in the last weeks of the year because I had read my students a poem by Langston Hughes. (His poems were banned in the Boston schools, as I was told when I was fired by my principal. But that's another story.) I turned to the superintendent of the Newton schools and asked him if he had a place for me in the Metco program. He assigned me to teach a fifth grade class in one of the schools that Metco kids attended. In addition to the Metco children at that school, there were also a number of Black students whose families had lived in a nearby neighborhood for several generations.

I asked the principal if I could set aside the traditional curriculum in geography and history in order to introduce my class to a unit about Africa. It was a time when African nations were freeing themselves of colonial rule. New nation names were appearing on the map as the European rulers were progressively expelled. So, with the help of two of my students who stayed late after school one day, I made a huge, wall-sized map—simply an empty outline of the continent. And then, from week to week, children would fill in the borders between nations, do independent research to locate different cities, fill in the names of major rivers, identify tribal and linguistic groups, and do some simple mathematics to estimate the distance between, for example, Kenya and Morocco.

The project was not particularly political, although some of the children would surprise me by bringing in stories from newspapers that alluded to rebellions, in Algeria for instance. All I really wanted was to stir the children's interest in a cultural arena that typically got short shrift in the textbooks of that era. It seemed to work. We had a ladder in the room, which I had placed in front of the Africa map. The children would take their turns climbing up high enough to add the information they were gathering.

None of this would have been possible if the school had not allowed us enough unrationed time for the kids to do their research and enjoy the independence I was giving them. I wanted the children in that class to come into school on Monday mornings with excitement about learning. In studying science, we were using a unit in which the kids used batteries and wires and some kits I bought at Radio Shack to understand electric currents. One of the boys made a crystal radio that actually brought in voices from a local station. The students also read a lot of poetry (I introduced them to Langston Hughes and Emily Dickinson and e. e. cummings and Robert Frost and Gwendolyn Brooks' poems about Chicago). They also wrote their own poems and interviewed their parents and grandparents to write stories about their families and ancestors.

The principal liked to come into the room and listen and applaud when the children read their poetry. She could be strict about the teaching of the basic skills, but she was also a gloriously independent spirit. She wanted the children to be happy.

One of the students in the class told me, about a year ago, that virtually all of her former classmates, as best she can recall, went on to college after high school, with the exception of two students from the neighborhood who went into job-training programs. One of the Metco students, who sends me Christmas cards each year, has had a long career as a senior executive in technology development. Two of the other Metco students—both of them boys whom I first met in Roxbury—went on to law school after college. Their success was not unusual.

In view of its impressive record over the course of nearly sixty years, an obvious question may be asked: Why have a great many more than 3,100 children not been admitted to the program up to now? What has been preventing a vast expansion of the program?

In the suburbs to the west and north and south of Boston that participate in Metco, there are nearly 110,000 students attending public schools. If the number of Metco students were to be increased at least three-fold, or four-fold, or maybe somewhat more, they would still represent only a modest fraction of the children in those schools. It's hard to believe that an additional 10,000 or 15,000 students in an expanded Metco program would lead to the fearsome prospect of white flight. To what destination would white families flee if they were so inclined? Would they abandon their lives in proximity to Boston and move to Northern Maine?

In any event, I don't believe white families in these districts would think the sky is falling if their children went to class with more than token numbers of Black and Latino children. I don't believe that parents are the problem in this instance.

The problem is resistance from political elites who cling to a racial status quo with which they are quite comfortable.

The state, after all, has always had the power to allocate the funding to compensate the suburbs for the added costs they would incur from admitting far more applicants, not only to create more classroom space and pay for transportation, but also to reinforce the efforts of those districts to develop policies and practices that are culturally inclusive. But chronic underfunding has always been a problem and, despite a recent increment in funding from the state, it's barely enough to keep up with present needs.

The Metco leadership and a new generation of determined advocates and parents have not given up the struggle to overcome resistance. New strategies are brewing to open up more doors. The parents know the challenges that children in this program, and other programs like it, often face. They still believe it's worth the ride. They think their kids can handle it. If we're ever going to dare to speak of reparations in the world of education—not as ineffectual parlor conversation, but in realistic terms—battering down the walls that lock so many children into poorly funded and unhappy and perennially unsuccessful schools of racial isolation would be a good beginning.

6

Culture and Identity

All over America, every morning, for five days every week, we see the blinking lights of the yellow bus that's picking up schoolchildren. At two or three p.m., we see the lights again as the bus returns the children to their neighborhood. Many of us plan our shopping trips in order to avoid sitting in our cars, stuck behind the bus, while little kids are climbing on and off and waving to their friends.

That good old familiar yellow bus has never posed a problem in our national perceptions except when it carried children of color across the lines of class and race out of the neighborhoods where they live into the better-funded schools of mainly white communities. In spite of the gains achieved in programs such as Metco, the stigma that attaches to that three-letter word continues to be with us in too many metro areas.

The same stigma also inhibits national leaders in Congress and the White House from taking a strong and ethical position to reinforce and replicate successful busing programs by using the power of the federal purse to incentivize the suburbs when funding by states has not been available. The refusal of those national leaders to contemplate any intervention of this nature is one of the most abiding obstacles to bringing children of different races together in their classrooms.

President Biden, sad to say, had an influential role in placing a taint on busing when he was in the Senate. "I oppose busing," he told a Delaware newspaper in 1975. "It's an asinine concept, the utility of which has never been proven to me. I've gotten to the point where I think our only recourse to eliminate busing may be a constitutional amendment." In 1977, he wrote to Senator James Eastland to express his thanks for Eastland's support of anti-busing legislation he had introduced. "I very much appreciate your help . . . ," Biden said to Eastland. When he was running for election in 2019, The New York Times described him as "the Anti-Busing Democrat."

Loyal mainstream Democrats have done their best to circumvent or talk away Mr. Biden's opposition to the one and only way of achieving integration within the public schools in a nation in which residential segregation continues unabated. The president has been widely praised by liberals for placing more Black faces in high places in the nation's governance, but this has yet to make a noticeable difference for millions of Black and Latino children who remain in isolation. And, although he insists that he's in favor of "fostering diversity"— and although his administration has recently provided the very modest sum of $12.5 million, to be shared among a dozen states, to further that objective—the president has said nothing, up to now, to indicate that he has overcome his irrational antipathy to letting children ride that yellow bus in order to go to a good suburban school.

Other, more reflective and knowledgeable critics of inter-district programs who believe, in principle, in the worth of integration often make the argument that it isn't fair to place the burden of cross-district busing on children from the cities while white kids in receiving districts remain in schools within their own communities. Why, they ask, should children of color be obliged to wake up early and spend perhaps an hour riding on a bus with no equivalent burden required of their classmates in the school that they're attending? It's an inescapable question and cannot be passed by lightly, even if the answer is painfully self-evident. Nobody's going to ride a bus into a failing and poorly funded district if they have a first-rate school right there in their neighborhood.

There are ways, however, to even out the balance, at least to some degree, by creating schools with strong magnetic power within or on the edges of an urban district in order to entice suburban children to make the same ride in reverse. In an area like Boston, for example, with its many universities and cultural centers—and I'm thinking also of its famous research hospitals—schools affiliated with these institutions might become a common ground for kids who come from opposite directions. Students of color living in the city and their counterparts from surrounding districts who aspire to careers in bioscience, for example, or dance and musical performance, or the study of art history, would, I am convinced, see beyond the differences in race and economic class between them in pursuit of learning goals they share.

Creating a ribbon of exciting schools like these while also expanding the present Metco program would obviously cost a lot more money than the state, up to now, has been prepared to spend. Still, there are signs here in Massachusetts that the tide may now be turning, although very slowly. Some of the media in Boston, which have often been ambivalent about the merits of cross-district busing, pointing to the occasional instances of openly voiced bigotry to which I have alluded, and casting a cold or cloudy eye at its remarkable achievements, seem to have begun to shed their doubts about the value of the program.

Over the past few years, the cautiously liberal Boston Globe has been running scathing stories on the persistent and increasing racial segregation of the Boston schools and drawn renewed attention to the inter-district program without the reservations it has sometimes voiced in decades past. An editorial and opinion writer at the paper, David Scharfenberg, recently noted that "here in Massachusetts . . . , the number of 'intensely segregated' nonwhite schools has grown by more than one-third in the last decades alone" and that "the political class has shown no sign of urgency" about this. This, he says, is "especially disappointing," in view of the "extraordinarily successful"—but, he adds, "too limited"—"experiment with the . . . program known as Metco."

Students in Metco, he goes on, drawing on numbers provided by the state, "dramatically outperform students with similar demographic profiles" in the Boston system—"with high school graduation and college enrollment rates about thirty percentage points higher." As he also notes, white students in these integrated schools "see no decline" in their performance. Given all this, "you'd think Massachusetts lawmakers would be eyeing a major expansion of Metco. But it's been a challenge just to maintain funding for the existing program."

Any attempt to integrate the Boston system "entirely from within" would, he adds, be "impossible" because so few white students remain in Boston's schools. "What I'm suggesting, instead, is a lawsuit that would build a bridge between Boston's mostly Black and brown students and their mostly white and Asian peers in the suburbs," relying upon an expanded Metco program and well-resourced magnet schools.

The Massachusetts Constitution, Scharfenberg observes, guarantees equal protection for all children in the public schools. It also provides for a level of education that can qualify as "adequate." The definition of "adequate," unfortunately, has always been subjected to political debate and, in the states that use that term, is typically pegged at a good deal less than "equal." But forcing the issue in the courts is strategically appealing.

I've cited Scharfenberg at length because his belief that equal education cannot be achieved without desegregation parallels my own but, more to the point, because his reasoned argument carries the authority of one of New England's most respected and most influential organs of opinion. Scharfenberg cites the director of the Boston-based Lawyers for Civil Rights, who believes that "lawyers from prominent Boston law firms would be eager to work on this . . . pro bono." If he's right, it would mark a major breach in the ranks of the city's corporate establishment.

The question remains: What is to be done in order that children of color in programs such as Metco will not have to pay the unacceptable price of losing their sense of cultural identity in a sea of whiteness?

One answer, obviously, would be to assure that more than a smattering of Black ands Latino children are assigned to any given school, so that they can turn to one another for mutual support when, or if, they sense that they're being disrespected. This is why, if Metco is to be substantially expanded, I would argue that, apart from attempting to add more suburbs, we ought to be placing more of these students in schools that are already receiving Metco children.

At the level of instruction, what adaptations in the content of curriculum and the consciousness of teachers can be rightfully expected? What kinds of adaptations have already been seen or, at least, earnestly attempted?

One essential adaptation—which has not gone nearly far enough—is to take more ambitious and more determined measures to recruit a great many more than token numbers of Black and Latino faculty and counselors. I have spoken of several Metco students whom I knew when they were starting school who, like Julia Walker's son, went on to be teachers in the district they'd attended or in other districts in the Boston area. The recruitment of former students as members of a faculty is, admittedly, a tiny step in the direction of faculty diversity. But it's one realistic way of opening a pipeline into the profession. Other, far less random and more systematic ways of recruiting Black and Latino faculty need to be at the top of any list of national priorities.

School integration, in any event, when it's accompanied by an exacting scrutiny of traditional curricula and an organized effort to be certain that the teaching of the arts and social sciences is no longer sanitized by obvious omissions, does not need to lead to the abandonment or thinning-out of any child's cultural identity. And, as I've seen in a number of schools, it often opens up a healthy and unhurried opportunity for children from different backgrounds to take a searching look at the nation's racial history as it bleeds into our present-day realities.

In one of the suburban districts that participate in Metco, I walked into a fourth grade class where children were immersed in a yearlong project about the civil rights uprisings in the 1960s. Two of the boys—one was Black, one was white—were working together on their essays, "doing the Greensboro movement," the Black student told me. My memory failed me for a moment. I asked if that was where John Lewis was arrested. "No," he said. "That was Nashville. This was Greensboro." And he showed me the names of the Greensboro students "who were known as the Greensboro Four," he said.

Civil rights was on the minds of other children at the school. In the stacks of books I saw in almost every room, there were far more titles about race and racial justice than I tend to see in deeply segregated inner-city schools, where the pressure on teachers to pump their students' scores by the methods we have seen leaves little time for allowing children to explore these social issues. (It's also understandable that principals and teachers in a segregated district tend to be reluctant to open up discussions about the dual system that their school exemplifies.) Ironically, as a result, in segregated schools, segregation tends to be less frequently discussed or openly confronted than in the integrated and more progressive schools, where no one's counting down the seconds before the next "transition."

I've also been in integrated schools in sections of a college town where faculty children go to class with children of color who live nearby in low-income neighborhoods. In a small Virginia city about a two-hour drive from Washington, I visited a school with a remarkable mix of students, where the principal and teachers and some members of the college faculty had worked together to develop a climate of instruction in which diversity was treated as a learning opportunity. Approximately ten percent of the children were African American. Another, significantly larger number were children of Latino parents who worked at local poultry farms and plants that packaged poultry. There were also a number of children who were recent immigrants from African and Middle Eastern nations. The remaining students, about twenty-five percent, were white children from the college families.

While I was observing a ninth grade class, a girl whose head was covered with a scarf was whispering to other girls, also wearing head scarfs, almost right in front of me. She was from Angola. The teacher didn't seem to be disturbed. When I leaned down closer, I realized that she wasn't speaking English. She was a multilingual child and was translating the teacher's words to the other girls, who didn't yet know English.

The teacher's recruitment of this child to serve, in a sense, as his assistant teacher seemed to have lent her a poised and quiet confidence. It struck me as a beautiful example of looking for the gifts that children bring us, no matter what their ethnic origins—or, as in this case, *because* of those origins. If this could be done in a comfortable way with a newly arrived student from Angola, it's hard to know why any school with a mix of kids who come from different backgrounds should see it as a formidable challenge to treat those kids respectfully.

At the end of the class, I saw the student from Angola chatting with a bunch of the local girls as they headed for the lunchroom. Crossing lines of race and class is not some kind of miracle. When we give them half a chance, children do it easily.

7

Education Without Fear

In making the argument for school desegregation, advocates and scholars frequently remind us of the academic gains that children of color were able to achieve during the period, beginning in the late 1960s and early 1970s, when court-ordered integration was seriously enforced in many central cities for almost twenty years. The achievement gap, as Hannah-Jones has noted, was reduced by roughly half during those hopeful years.

In this book, I've pointed to other measurable gains that continue to be seen in integration efforts like the one in metro Boston—the stunning graduation rates and the rates of college admission and enrollment, to give two obvious examples. But it's not so much these compelling numbers with which I've been primarily concerned. It's the world of difference in environments of learning between the relatively open-ended and less tension-ridden education that continues to be favored in good suburban schools and, at the other extreme, a pressure-cooker ethos of tightly scripted training, an often morbid code of discipline, and coercive uniformity.

When a state board of education tells us that one school or district can claim to be "successful," while another one cannot, I think we have the right to question how that word has been defined. Does the happiness of children have any place at all in our estimation of a school's success or failure? Would we call a school successful if its students' scores did not improve by leaps and bounds in any given year, but if the children made reasonable progress in their skills and also gained a greater sense of empathy and moral generosity to other children in the school who may be less competitive than they? (Is value added to the child if she or he becomes more kind to other children?) In a nation torn apart by class and racial fears and episodic waves of violence that seem beyond control, how many points do teachers get for doing all they can to give their kids a chance not just to be respectful of each other but to value and enjoy the differences between them? How many extra points do teachers get for giving kids the message that life in school does not need to be a headlong race to outdo one another or to prove how "useful" and "productive" they will someday be, maybe twenty years from now, in the eyes of an economist?

Children spend something like six or seven hours in their classrooms every day, five days a week, for forty or more weeks a year, for thirteen years, a total of approximately 18,000 hours if they stay in high school long enough to graduate. If they repeat a grade or two or are required to remain in school for afternoon tutorials to drill them for their next exam, it's probably more than 20,000 hours. That's a good big chunk of anyone's existence. Are all those days and years and hours to be seen as little more than basic training for utilitarian adulthood? Does the present tense of childhood have no inherent value of its own?

When I'm in a class of children who are maybe eight or nine years old, it's always in my mind that they will never have a second chance to live this year of childhood again. This is it. They get it once and then it's gone forever. Denying those children the right to find some fear-free satisfaction in the years they're living in the here and now is an ultimate act of theft because it's irreversible.

At one of the New York City charter schools that are part of the charter chain known as Success Academy, a child grew confused in explaining to her teacher how she got an answer on a mathematics problem. According to a video recorded in the classroom and given to Kate Taylor of The New York Times, the teacher took the child's paper in her hands and ripped it up in front of her. At another school that's part of the same charter chain, children were trained in a strategy for taking tests that was known as "the plan of attack." A student who forgot or failed to use the plan of attack, according to The Times, was sent into a place of detention that was known as "Effort Academy."

"We can NOT let up on them . . . ," teachers at the school were told in an email from a teacher-leader cited by The Times. "This is serious business. . . . There has to be misery felt for the kids who are not doing what is expected of them."

The idea that misery must be felt by children in order to learn successfully and meet our expectations is one of those atrocious notions that would likely stir a storm of protest in almost any of the better schools in mainly white and affluent districts that I know firsthand. Parents and teachers in those schools would not accept this suffering.

There is so much suffering in this world already without the addition of intentional immiseration. No matter what our race or class, we all have to face the fear of serious disease and the continuing contagion of the viral epidemic, not to speak of the perils that we face at the hands of armed invaders in our schools and public places and the environmental perils from which no one is protected and are certain to grow greater in the decade now ahead.

Why, then, compound these griefs by piling on manu-factured miseries in any public school or charter school, no matter by what twisted logic they are held to be "effective" in the teaching of young children of one specific class and color? This, in my own belief, is perhaps the most commanding rea-son why I think we ought to give these children every chance we can to escape the "serious business" of force-fed education and enable them to go to schools where the human rights of childhood are more faithfully defended.

In saying this, I'm hearkening back to one of the most enlightened and delightful—and desegregated—schools that I've had the joy of visiting. According to a third grade teacher at the school, some of the usual standardized demands could not be totally avoided. "We have to give the state exams. We have no choice about that. But we don't drill them all year long. We don't think we need to."

The teacher was one of those cheerful souls who see no need to choose between the "delivery" of essential skills and the day-to-day well-being of their students while they're learning. In order to make the children feel as relaxed and comfortable as possible, she had arranged the room to look like a living room. There was a big blue sofa in the middle of the room and six or seven wicker chairs, painted white, that looked as though they might belong on the front porch of a mansion in the Hamptons or on the coast of Maryland. Smaller chairs were scattered here and there around a long, low maple table and a rocking chair. There were also some of the usual desks and tables that you'd see in any public school but, when I walked into the classroom, the children were not sitting at those tables. Some of them were curled up on the sofa or sitting in the wicker chairs doing silent reading, while others were sprawled out across a reading rug working together on a complicated project with colored rods and boxes that they were assembling into structures they'd designed that called for careful measurement.

"It's going to be a bridge that goes across a river," a boy with braided hair explained to me. "If we do it wrong, the cars go in the water!" The teacher laughed and touched him on the shoulder. A white boy sitting next to him put his finger on the bridge to see if it was strong enough. . . .

I told the teacher, "If I could be a child again, I'd love to be a student here." I watched as the children did their work, singly or together, as the teacher moved around the room, stooping down now and then if a child had a question or to see if a book a child was reading was perhaps too hard for her. All in all, it was a safe small world where the children were thoroughly immersed in learning without the need for threats and warnings. If we're in search of success in education, I think this classroom with its big blue sofa—and those two little boys working together on their bridge across a river—would be a beautiful example.

In a courtyard of that school, framed by three walls of the building, there was a garden with flowering plants and little tables, or "workstations," dotted here and there. I later saw some of the children from that teacher's class sitting together at one of those tables, working on a lesson the teacher had assigned, next to a huge sunflower plant. I didn't ask what they were writing. I simply watched and thought: This is the kind of happy and life-affirming school that need not be unusual.

Those who are attracted by the pleasant informality of the teacher in the room with the blue sofa are easily dismissed as out-of-touch progressives who have never grown beyond our old attachment to the values of Fred Rogers and the gentle and uplifting world of learning he created. If that's the accusation, I don't take it as an insult. If we're looking for a model for teachers of young children, I'd opt for Mr. Rogers anytime before I'd look to tough guys with their penalties and paddles.

Letting children ride a bus into a more humane and child-centered district with a whole lot more resources is obviously no magic pill that guarantees they're going to be free from times of tension in the course of class instruction. But, in the hopeful settings that I've seen, it's a lot more likely they'll be spared from the less than lovely ethos that so frequently prevails, with all its crackpot slogans and repeated cycles of "reform," in the schools they've left behind. If it also gives them greater opportunities to pursue their curiosities, a richer range of studies in a less restrictive menu, and a chance to ask more unpredicted and unscripted questions to each other and the teacher, those are added reasons to open up the doors between austerity and plenitude, gratuitous unhappiness and now and then some time for normal fun and laughter.

In speaking as I did nostalgically of the values of Fred Rogers, I was thinking of the time we spent together visiting with children in a South Bronx neighborhood about six years before he passed away. The severity agenda was beginning to be accepted and embedded as the regimen of choice for Black and Latino children in their public schools. Mr. Rogers' way of being with young children was, of course, entirely different. He had a gift for bringing out the voices and opinions of children who may have been shy with him at first. He would squeeze himself into one of those little chairs and ask the children questions, and he liked it when they rambled on and he listened to them patiently. I wish he were still with us to remind us about listening.

8

Batter Down the Walls

Far from the safe and reassuring world of Mr. Rogers' neighborhood, and far from the classroom with the big blue sofa, back in the districts in which this book began, the disparate agenda lingers on, the dire admonitions and punitive protocols continue to prevail, and the buildings too often are still in shameful disrepair.

But the perception of children of color as the victims of a racist social order raises the hackles of certain of my critics, who deplore the lens of victimhood because they think it runs directly counter to the goal of developing positive thinking among teachers and an ethos of self-help among the children. "Don't think of them as victims. Think of them as stalwart little champions who, if they show sufficient effort, can rise above it all. . . ."

It's a delicate dilemma. If we cannot speak of victims, if the word is in disfavor, what other language can be used to speak of children who are faced with cognitive suppression in almost every aspect of instruction, not to speak of physical assault, rituals of shaming, lockdowns in a hallway closet and, too often, toxic dangers to their health? Then, too, if there are no victims, then no crime has been committed. If no crime has been committed, there can be no reason for demanding redress for what these children undergo in their schools of sequestration. Avoiding a disfavored word cannot expunge reality.

There are also those who would probably dismiss much of the emphasis I have placed on race and racist practices in the public schools on the grounds that race, in their belief, is no longer a "fundamental determinant" in the allocation of the nation's blessings or in their denial. Instead, they say, it is primarily economic class, as opposed to race, that determines these inequities. "An obsession with disparities of race has colonized the thinking of left and liberal types," as the writer and political scientist Adolph Reed has stated in an interview with The New York Times. In another, considerably longer interview in 2022, recorded on video under the title "Race and Class After American Segregation," he fiercely rejected what he believes to be "a kind of luxuriation in a romanticized fantasy of suffering" on the part of people of color.

I have always looked to Mr. Reed as one of the great Black scholars and advocates for democratic justice of my generation. But, on this matter of an allegedly declining significance of race, I am compelled to disagree. As someone who has spent thousands of hours in our schools in the course of my career, and has returned to many of those schools over recent years, and has seen the effects of the punitive agenda as it has been artfully refined, I have to wonder what is meant by a "fantasy of suffering."

White students in very poor or working-class communities are often treated harshly and unfairly too, but the racial differentials are too great and obvious to be blithely set aside, as if the indignities and miseries Black and Latino children have to face are only marginally related to the color of their skin. The nearly total isolation of those children, in any case, cannot be explained by poverty alone. Many families here in Boston's Black community who are by no means wealthy but who earn a decent living have nonetheless had to see their children slotted into poorly funded, physically unpleasant, and academically unsuccessful schools that have long been abandoned by the children of white people.

Inner-city principals and other school officials with whom I've worked for years are unlikely to agree that we are living in an era "after" segregation—they see the truth every day right there before their eyes. Some, however, see no reason to take issue with a system that creates these demographics. I'm thinking, for example, of certain urban principals who invite me to their schools and see me as an ally and a friend, but who really do believe that Black and Latino children have uniquely "different" needs and that those needs can best be met in rigorous but separate schools. Some go even further and, in a quiet moment at the end of school or perhaps over dinner if I'm staying for the evening, will tell me that the drive for integration in the decades after *Brown* may have done more harm than good, because it did away with schools in which, they say, Black parents, principals, and teachers had some degree of power to educate Black children in ways that they thought best.

As a white man and a teacher of that generation who worked at a school where the parents of my students and the few Black teachers had virtually no power, I don't know what to say. I have been privileged, after all, by the trust and camaraderie with which I've been treated by these seasoned principals. It feels too much like a breach of faith to question their convictions and their sense of history. So I nod and listen and try to be respectful, even while I deeply disagree.

I had a long and stirring conversation with John Lewis, the late congressman from Georgia, a little more than twenty years ago, in which he made it clear that he found this line of thinking not only unconvincing but a disappointing throwback to the era when he was a child in Pike County, Alabama. My conversation with the congressman took place in his office after a meeting of the Congressional Black Caucus, to which he invited me to speak about the schools in Northern cities that I had been visiting. He began our conversation by speaking of the ruling of the Warren court in *Brown v. Board of Education.*

"I remember 1954," he said. "I was fourteen years old at the time." When he heard about the court's decision, he recalled that he felt almost jubilant. "I actually believed that we would have school integration before long. I was so hopeful and optimistic. . . .

"Now segregation seems almost to be the order of the day. We don't have many people who believe that integration's even possible or worth attempting anymore, not in the government at least. You don't hear it from the president"—he was referring to then-president George W. Bush—"or other leaders here in Washington. You don't hear it being mentioned in political campaigns. . . ."

I told him of the principals with whom I had been speaking, who had turned away, it seemed, from any further efforts to pursue the goals of *Brown.* The congressman nodded quickly. "I sometimes say, 'They've had an executive session with themselves.' They've sort of decided, 'It's not gonna happen. I've given up. I don't have the strength or energy to fight it anymore. . . .'" Saying this, he clenched his fingers into fists, but with his index fingers out, and seemed to stab the air.

Separatist agendas that extol the benefits of segregated schools stirred a passionate reaction from the congressman, and he rejected flatly the idea that segregated schools in olden days in the Southern states were something to be recollected with nostalgia. "That's nonsense," he replied. " 'Yes, in the 1930s and the 1940s we had good segregated schools with no white children . . . in the South.' This is nonsense," he repeated. He told me of the "schools for coloreds" that Black children had attended when he was a boy. He had spent his high school years at Pike County Training School for Coloreds, while white students of his age attended schools that offered a more far-reaching and entirely different level of expansive opportunities. Any attempt to romanticize the dual system of those days or the modern version of that system in our present age was, he said, unthinkable.

He didn't limit himself to the familiar arguments about unequal funding in a segregated system. He wasn't speaking solely of inadequate resources. "This nation," he said, "needs to be a family, and a family sits down for its dinner at a table, and we all deserve a place together at that table. And our children deserve to have a place together in their schools and classrooms. . . .

"No matter what the present mood in Washington is like, no matter what the people who are setting policy today believe, or want us to believe, no matter what the sense of temporary hopelessness that many of us feel, we cannot give up on the struggle we began and on the dream that brought us here."

When Lewis passed away at the age of eighty in 2020, he was widely honored as a peaceful warrior for justice. His words about "good trouble" were frequently repeated at memorial events and were cited by Joe Biden, who was then in the midst of his electoral campaign. The words may have had a reassuring sound because "good trouble" in itself, when taken out of context, didn't sound too threatening. But we didn't hear much, if anything at all, about his strong belief that integration in our public schools "still remains the goal worth fighting for." Inconvenient pieces of a fallen warrior's beliefs are easily deleted or lightly painted over when they represent a danger to our equanimity.

The challenge to that equanimity that John Lewis posed throughout the course of his career has been taken up again in recent years by many of the young Black activists, some of them barely out of high school, who do not accept that race is suddenly a secondary factor in the way they are perceived and treated. The strange idea that race may now be taken off the table when we talk about disparities may be a consoling thought to those who actually believe this, but almost every day we see alarming evidence, not only in our schools but wholly beyond the realm of education, that this is an appeasing self-deception.

As I am writing, the suppression of voting rights for Black

and Latino citizens in dozens of states governed by Republicans has dragged us back to the days before the Voting Rights Act of 1965, while the 2021 John Lewis Voting Rights Advancement Act, after it was passed in the House of Representatives, was blocked in the Senate by conservative refusal to set aside the filibuster. Meanwhile, again and again in recent years, we have seen the spectacle of Black teenagers and adults subjected to abuse and killings at the hands of the police. They are not hounded down and killed because, or if, they're poor. They are abused or killed because of where they live and the color of their skin.

At the same time, as we can see more vividly now than ever because of images caught by smartphone cameras and then broadcast on TV, immigration policies are wildly racist too. White immigrants from European nations are typically welcomed to our shores—not only those in need of urgent rescue, as in the case of people fleeing the invasion in Ukraine, but also those who come here as students at our universities or simply to advance in their careers. No such welcome has been accorded to desperate families and their children coming here from Mexico and other Latin nations—nor to those who come here to escape disease and hunger and political oppression in the tortured land of Haiti. The image of Haitian children being whipped back into the river at the Texas border by U.S. agents riding horses stirred a sense of outrage among many decent people, but, since that time, the government has been shipping Haitian families by the planeload back into the terrors they were fleeing.

Our continuing lack of mercy for immigrants of color is one more stark reminder of the festering racist sickness in our nation's character. The consignment of children of color to schools of desolation is not in the same ballpark of obvious brutality as our immigration policies, but there's a not-so-slender thread between the two indecencies. Doing away, at long last, with those age-old barriers that make our children strangers to each other, and too often fearful of each other, would be at least one good big step in a civilized direction.

I realize it's unlikely, given my age, that I'm going to live to see a fulfillment of this dream on any vast and sweeping scale. But the vision of John Lewis—"this nation needs to be a family" and our children "deserve to have a place together at the table"—need not be a wistful dream. It's within our power to make it real if we ever have the will and find the courage to begin to heal our self-inflicted wounds.

9

A Letter to the Future

This will be a message to all the many good, hardworking teachers of young children I have known—it must be several thousand by this time—who have brought me to their classrooms and often still reach out to me today to tell me of the challenges and disappointments that they face. Many of those teachers who have come to education with a background in the arts and letters speak of their frustration with curricular demands that diminish the place of the humanities in the course of class instruction and limit the time in which their students can immerse themselves in literary works—poetry and fiction—not for the sake of tests they will be given, but for the enjoyment of those writings in themselves. They also speak of the dwindling number of librarians and the absence of school libraries in which their students can poke around and pick out titles that appeal to them.

The loss of school librarians tells the tale succinctly. In New York City, the number of school librarians declined from nearly 1,500 in 2005 to 450 in 2022, leading to a ratio of approximately one librarian to more than 2,000 students. In Los Angeles, there is one school librarian for every 4,345 students. In Chicago, more than 400 schools, including more than eighty percent of elementary schools, have no school librarian.

Cleveland does a good deal better than many urban districts (one librarian to 1,536 students), while Detroit does considerably worse (one librarian to more than 24,000 students). In Boston, there is one school librarian for 6,700 students, which may be compared to the ratio in suburban Newton (one to about 600) and in Cambridge (one to about 300).

Racial and economic differentials in the student population of a school or district correlate closely with the presence or the absence of librarians and libraries. In Chicago, only ten percent of schools in which Black children make up the largest proportion of the student population still have school librarians, according to an investigative study published in 2021 and cited in a lengthy piece of disturbing reportage by the Chicago Sun-Times in 2022. Nationwide, schools with the largest enrollments of low-income children and minority children, as well as schools in rural districts, are those that are most likely to have no librarians.

But the overall trend of abandoning school libraries, and the role of librarians to guide the children through them, is part of the larger pattern of retreat from the humanities in general, and the arts and letters in particular, which tend to be given less and less attention, as it seems, because the benefits or "outcomes" of a child's engagement with a literary work that he or she enjoys do not easily lend themselves to rigorous and scientific measurement.

All of this began to be apparent a little more than twenty years ago at the time when the misleadingly titled No Child Left Behind was enacted into law. "I want to change the face of reading instruction from an art to a science," said a high-ranking official at the U.S. Department of Education in 2002. If she had simply meant that reading instruction ought to be grounded in reputable research with a scientific basis, her statement would have seemed like common sense to me. Unhappily, in too many schools, the scientific theme soon grew into a storm of Arctic air that blew away any serious concern for the artistry of language in the books and stories that children were increasingly denied the time to read.

Subtracting the arts from English Language Arts soon had its repercussions in schools throughout the nation. In the elementary grades, in classes I observed, children were reading fewer books, whether classics or more modern titles. Instead, they were learning out-of-context reading skills from tiny chunks of test-aligned materials that were called "text passages."

"So maybe we aren't teaching an entire novel," a curriculum administrator in a New York district noted in an interview with The New York Times in 2015, "but we're ensuring that we're teaching the concepts that the novel would have gotten across."

It's a funny statement. I don't think too many people read

a novel in order to dig out "a concept" or a bunch of concepts hidden in its pages. I think most people read a novel to enjoy the story and get caught up in the lives of the people it portrays and the ways their personalities and character develop as the narrative evolves. All of this is pretty near impossible if all the students get to read are a couple paragraphs or pages.

There are, of course, notable exceptions to this unhappy pattern, more often than not in the wealthier and more progressive districts where principals and parents would tend to roll their eyes at the idea of sending children on a "concept hunt" in bits of books that they never got to read. But schools like these are less likely to be found in inner-city districts and in working-class communities, where the reading of books for the sake of "the book" has increasingly been left to the margins of instruction, sometimes at the tail end of the day or week, if the children ever get to them at all.

A case in point: One of the bright young teachers whom I came to know when she was a graduate student here in Cambridge went on a few years later to become a teacher in a fifth grade classroom in a district in Virginia. There was no library at the school and, in the classrooms, literary books had largely been abandoned and replaced by what she called "hokey little bits and pieces"—a reference to the practice texts. Even more disheartening, she said, many of these pieces had not been written by real authors, not at least by anyone she said she'd ever heard of, but, as she surmised, had been written or adapted by curriculum committees.

Each passage, the teacher said, was followed by a bubble-test like the ones that would appear on the standardized exams for which this was preparing them. The passages had been selected to set up the questions they would have to answer. It occurred to me that the people who served on these committees must have spent a lot of time creating or selecting these materials. But the teacher said that some of these passages had already been used in tests that had been given to other fifth grade students a year or two before.

The teacher, who had studied education after she had done her undergraduate degree in modern poetry and fiction, had done her practice teaching in a relatively progressive district in a suburb close to Cambridge where testing pressures had been less severe and where she'd had a chance to introduce her students to books she'd known and loved since she was a child. So the idea of using amputated pieces of test-aligned materials as the mainstay of instruction struck her, as she put it, as "pretty damn amazing."

The passages her children had to read included fiction and nonfiction and one piece of poetry. In the case of the nonfiction passages, according to the instructions she'd been given, children were expected "to demonstrate comprehension of nonfiction texts" but were also expected to "use reading strategies throughout the reading process to monitor comprehension," which sounds like something different and distinct from simple comprehension because it calls for "strategies." The notion of "monitoring" reading comprehension throughout the act of comprehending was, she said, "gobbledygook to me," but was apparently intended to sound scientific, even if it seemed redundant and perplexing to the teacher.

She later sent me a package that included several of the passages her students had to read in a six-week period prior to the final round of standardized exams—during which, she told me, they read no books at all. "I hated myself for doing this. I'd brought in a stack of books, novels mostly, but we never got to them until the testing stuff was over. . . ."

One of the pieces that she sent was a passage of nonfiction about a creature of the sea I had never heard of, which was called the blobfish. It started out by saying that the blobfish has "a human-looking face" and, in the next sentence, is "a human-looking fish" and, in the paragraph that followed, is "nearly human-looking." While it "may not be one of the most attractive of sea creatures," the passage continues, "it is certainly one of the most interesting." Its shapelessness "allows the blobfish to float easily" in "the ocean depths where it makes its home." The blobfish "spends all its time floating" and, two sentences later, the blobfish (plural) "spend most of their time floating . . . They are made for floating."

The blobfish "may not be the most attractive fish," the children are told a second time in the final paragraph, after which a multiple-choice question asks the students to identify the structure that was used to organize the passage. The teacher said one of her students stuck her fingers in her throat to indicate how interesting she found this.

She also sent me a short piece of fiction, apparently intended to teach the children something about usages of adverbs and adverbial expressions—"Mrs. Barnes said jokingly," "with a cheery smile," "with a twinkle in her eye," "Charlie asked enthusiastically. . . ." The teacher said she thought that it was better written than The Blobfish, but she had to wonder why they couldn't find a story to show the students how to use an adverb or a modifying phrase without it sounding "so contrived and goofy."

She also sent the only poem her students were assigned. It was an old chestnut about the newspaper writer Nellie Bly that had a pounding and insistent rhyme. ("A daring young reporter / whose name was Nellie Bly / proposed to travel 'round the world / —she simply had to try!") The children, she said, found it "kind of corny" and she didn't linger on it long. In the final weeks of school, after the last exam, she read them works by poets that she liked—William Carlos Williams ("The Red Wheelbarrow") and Dylan Thomas, and Marge Piercy ("To Be of Use"), and Mary Oliver, and Nikki

Giovanni—on which she told them in advance they would not be tested.

It's not surprising that so many teachers with her good education and buoyant personality—and feisty resistance to the loss of her autonomy—are turning their backs on public schools and looking for more rewarding work where their gifts will be respected. The flight of teachers from our schools, especially from the urban schools, has been widely noted as a growing crisis in states throughout the nation. One of the reasons, obviously, is the insufficient scale of pay. Teachers in most public schools (in the elementary grades they're more often than not likely to be women) get so little pay that they often need to look for second jobs on weekends or at night or before school in the morning. But poor remuneration is not the only reason, and not the most common reason, that I hear when teachers tell me they're on the verge of quitting. It's the total package of cultural attrition, on top of the often dismal physical conditions, that lead so many to the point of leaving the profession.

The banning of books on social justice issues and works that address the nation's racial history is another reason why teachers who have come to education with a sense of social conscience are fleeing from the classrooms. About twelve years ago, one of my friends in Arizona told me of teachers in the Tucson district who had developed a Mexican American studies program that also included the writings of James Baldwin and dissident historians, like Howard Zinn for instance, who document the stories seldom told in textbooks that are handed out to children.

But legislative leaders were not pleased. The legislature passed a law to eliminate the program, and the Republican governor, Jan Brewer, signed the law in 2012. Among the titles taken from the shelves were works by Cesar Chavez, Isabel Allende, Sandra Cisneros, Laura Esquivel, Paulo Freire, Mumia Abu-Jamal (*Live From Death Row*), educational psychologist David Berliner, and Thoreau (*Civil Disobedience*)— and, bewilderingly enough, Shakespeare's play *The Tempest*. (My friend also told me that one of my own books, *Savage Inequalities*, had been taken from the shelves. He said, "You're in good company.")

In more recent years, conservative and far-right parent groups have been launching fierce attacks on hundreds of other books that foster critical thinking or address the conflicts that divide us, based on gender, class, and race. Principals and teachers who believe in the value of these books have been bitterly attacked at public school board meetings. All in all, between the assault from groups like these and the broader curricular constraint on reading almost any book of literary worth from the beginning to the ending, teachers I know are speaking of a bleak and bare scenario.

I go into a classroom and, being old-fashioned as I am, I look to see if *Harriet the Spy* is sitting there invitingly on the top shelf of a bookcase. Depending on the grade and ages of the students, I also look for *Owl Moon*, *Peeny Butter Fudge*, *Born on the Water*, *Bridge to Terabithia*, *Grandma's Purse*, *Gulliver's Travels*, *The Wind in the Willows*, *Number the Stars*, *A Wrinkle in Time*, Alice's adventures when she fell into the rabbit hole—and, naturally, Eeyore, Pooh, and Piglet as they were depicted not by Disney but by E.H. Shepard.

Most of these books and dozens of other old or modern treasures are usually listed by the state or district as recommended titles for kids of different ages, and they're usually there, somewhere in the classroom, packed in shelves or boxes. Too often, however, unless I'm in the kind of school where progressive values have survived and teachers are allowed some sensible autonomy, the books remain there in the shelves and boxes for too many days and hours while children fill in bubbles on their practice texts. Whether students read these texts on a sheet of paper passed out by the teacher or on a laptop or a tablet, it's a shallow and reductive exercise. The teachers I admire most tell me that they hate it. They did not come into teaching in order to become the dutiful technicians of mechanistic learning. They want to seed the future of their students with a lifelong love of reading.

The children's author Eric Carle once told me that he had

gone to school in Germany in the early 1940s and had suffered greatly from the grimly technocratic and autocratic teaching at his school in Munich. He hoped his books would light a spark of joy and whim for children in this nation. I hope that teachers of young children will help to keep that spark from dying and will try to heap the table of instruction with a feast of wonderment. It's harder to do this in the kinds of schools where whim and wonderment are not really wanted and playfulness in learning is considered a distraction. But, despite the discouragement that many of you feel, I hope you will stay there in the classrooms where our children need you.

Afterword: Author's Q and A

A number of my friends and colleagues have been reading portions of this book as I have been writing. Some of them have asked me questions in regard to certain issues I've addressed, but sometimes only passingly. Here are a few of their questions and my attempts to answer them.

Question: When you've spoken about "data" and the phrase you say you often hear—"according to the data that we have at hand"—you may seem to be dismissing the entire body of academic research and the empirical evidence that has seemed to lend support to policies and practices that you consider harmful and unsound.

Answer: What I intended to say, and continue to believe, is that the assembling of data is not always neutral, and the selective application of the data I was citing is often used to justify an autocratic ethos, as in those commandeering guidelines for "The Demanding Teacher." School officials in these cases typically claim that they are using "data-driven" strategies. I think we have the right to look very hard at the sources of that data, and not accept it blindly.

Question: In your earlier books and interviews you have usually joined the call for universal pre-K for three- and four-year-olds. We are still light years from that goal. Do you see any indications that universal pre-K may, at long last, be politically attainable?

Answer: Some of us have argued for so long for good and plentifully funded preschool education that I didn't want to beat that horse again. And, for now, as another recession is being dolefully predicted, and given the political makeup of the House and Senate, it's hard to believe that national leaders will suddenly do what they have failed to do before. More than a million eligible children are still unable to receive the benefits of the federal Head Start program. Similar programs funded by the states or local districts, with some notable exceptions, continue to be a scattershot approach. Too many children are still locked out, while privileged families often spend as much as $30,000 or $40,000 yearly to buy their children a golden opportunity that sets them on the path to advanced and gifted classes when they enter public school.

Meanwhile, many of the publicly funded programs I've observed in primarily Black or brown communities have been forced to adopt much of the test-and-drill mentality in order to get the children ready for the regimen of rigor and "acceptable behavior" that await them when they enter kindergarten and first grade. If we ever achieve the goal of universal pre-K, which has been promised now for decades by countless state and local politicians, as well as by a number of presidential candidates, the battle ahead will be to defend the right of children to be protected from the hammer blows of an ignorant agenda of destructive conscientiousness, as Erik Erikson worded this more than sixty years ago.

Question: It is generally believed that the teaching of phonics is one of the essential early phases of a literacy program. But the degree of emphasis to be placed on phonics has always been a matter of contentious disagreement. Do you care to enter the great debate on this?

Answer: Yes. I have always believed that the teaching of phonics ought to be a part of any reading program for children who have not already gained these skills before they enter school. And most of the teachers I've observed continue to teach phonics to their students in the early grades and consider this a quintessential starting point in teaching them to read. At the same time, I also believe that early exposure to enticing books of words and pictures ought to be a parallel activity. I'm thinking again of beautiful books like *Grandma's Purse*, and *Owl Moon*, and *Peeny Butter Fudge*. I've also seen young children drawn into the delightful world of *Lilly's Purple Plastic Purse*, the now-classic work of Kevin Henkes, even while they're learning how to sound out words like "Lilly," "purse," and "purple."

I see no reason why these and other charming works like

The Grouchy Ladybug and *The Tiny Seed*—two of the gifts that Eric Carle has left us—cannot coexist with a coherent emphasis on phonics. The teaching of phonics, in my own belief at least, need not be restricted to relentless drill. Some degree of pleasure in the artistry of language ought to be a part of it. But, in saying this, I'm drawing on my own experience with children. So you can write off my opinion if you disagree with me.

Question: Many schools in recent years have been adopting a body of practices, generally known as Restorative Justice, in order to cut down on the punitive practices that you described in Chapter Three. Have you any sense of how successful this has been?

Answer: Well, it's difficult to tell. In some districts, it's clearly been a helpful intervention—in the case of classroom bullying, for instance. Teachers or counselors or sometimes school psychologists mediate between the bullied and the bully and try to arrive at reconciliations in which the bully makes amends without the need for harsh, abusive penalties.

But many elementary schools lack the funds to hire counselors or retain a school psychologist on any routine basis, and, when they do have counselors, they are typically asked to serve the needs of at least 600 children. Then, too, the entire body of restorative practices, or what are known as "trauma-informed

approaches," has often been regarded as overly indulgent—
too "idealistic," too "progressive" ("touchy-feely" is a term
we've heard)—by its tough-minded critics. There's also been
a tendency, as a young Latina teacher put it to me at a conference at her school in Colorado, to relegate these programs to
what she called "insular" activities of "programmed sensitiv-
ity," a warm spot, as it were, within a cold terrain.

Still, when it's *not* an insular activity and is allowed to per-
vade the everyday experience of children in a school, it may
be reducing the harshness of the punitive approaches, like the
closet in the hallway, and suspensions and expulsions, and,
most important, the willingness to call in the police.

Question: The use of corporal punishment, however, continues to be legal, as you've noted, in nearly half the states,
and some of the most flagrant examples of its use continue to
appear in local media accounts. You've pointed to a Supreme
Court ruling in the 1970s that denied the protection of the
"cruel and unusual punishment" clause in the Eighth Amendment to children in our schools. In the absence of this constitutional protection, is there anything the federal government
can do to prohibit or reduce the frequency of this legalized
abuse?

Answer: There have been some hopeful indications. In the
spring of 2023, President Biden's Education Secretary, Miguel

Cardona, wrote to local school officials urging them to do away with this practice altogether. He noted that physical abuse of children, among its other damaging effects, is likely to heighten their aggressive inclinations. Violence to children may subdue them for a while, but it also leaves an imprint and sometimes a lasting lesson that may come back to haunt us: When all else fails in pursuit of an objective, the use of force and cruelty may seem to be legitimate alternatives. Is this a lesson that we want to teach our children in a nation that's too violent already?

Question: One of the obligations of any public school is to give its students the skills they're going to need when they're old enough to go to work in a competitive society. In your writing about the diminution of the arts and letters—poetry and fiction and artistry in general—it may appear that you're disregarding anything that smacks of what you call "utility." Is there any reason why we need to choose between realistic practicality on the one hand and, on the other hand, a full and rich exposure to the world of the humanities?

Answer: Competent teachers do not need to make that choice. They know that children need to be prepared to go out and earn a living when they're no longer children. The question that many of them ask, however, is whether students who are only six or eight or ten years old ought to be perceived as just so many economic units in a corporate society, and long before they're old enough to choose the kinds of lives they might like to lead and the work in which they might, or might not, find some satisfaction.

Vocational and job-specific education has always been an option for students in the upper grades of secondary school if they do not choose—or don't believe they can afford—to set their sights on higher education. But, even for those who are heading straight to work or to a technical training academy once they finish high school, I think their lives, as well as their ability to use their skills humanely, are going to be diminished if they were denied the cultural exposure that children of the privileged usually enjoy.

Wealthy and well-educated parents, as we've seen, have tended to resist this narrowing of focus—in part because they know that cultural breadth and stylistic confidence are class and social markers, "entry tickets," as it were, to many of the most rewarding levels of employment. Withholding that "ticket" from children of less empowered families is one more way in which we limit equal opportunity.

Question: The chapter in which you wrote about the presence of lead and other toxins in schools that have been left in disrepair was terribly disturbing. But I think that many people are going to assume that, in the wake of the increasing media attention that's been given to this problem in very recent years, it must have significantly diminished by this time. It just seems to be embedded in our character—I mean in our way of thinking as Americans—to want to believe that we are always making progress in correction of a problem that we have not corrected in the past.

Answer: Yes, I think this theme of inevitable progress is built into our culture. Unfortunately, there has been all too little progress in protecting children from lead and other toxins in the schools of many states and cities over the most recent years.

In California, more than half the districts that tested for lead poison found the water in their schools unsafe for kids to drink, according to a study by the California Public Interest Research Group in 2020. A follow-up study in 2023 found that the water in more than 2,000 fountains in the Los Angeles district and other districts in the state was still unsafe to drink. In Philadelphia, in 2022, "widespread lead contamination" was detected in at least one water outlet in almost every public school, according to a report from public radio WHYY, an NPR affiliate. (This was three years after The Inquirer had exposed the full dimensions of the problem in its series "Toxic City.") In 2019, "at least 94 . . . public schools in 30 districts of Tennessee," according to Chalkbeat, found high lead levels in their water, either in a drinking fountain

or in a sink that was used "for washing hands" or "to prepare food or clean dishes in [the] cafeterias." In the same year,
"nearly 1,000 classrooms serving [New York City's] youngest
students," as again reported by Chalkbeat, were found to have
"deteriorating" lead paint in their walls or ceilings.

The quiet devastation of the young mentalities of children,
and the racial differentials in those who are affected, continue
to mock the promises that political officials have routinely
made for decades—and repeatedly betrayed.

Question: In your reflections about Metco, you cite convincing evidence of the overwhelmingly successful outcomes
for kids who ride the bus to good suburban districts. Do you
have any thoughts about the benefits of this and similar programs to the kids who live in these mainly white communities?

Answer: Yes. And many of the parents in those districts,
at least the ones I personally know, recognize the benefits
their children have derived from learning together with children from a different culture than their own. Well-known
and respected scholars and researchers who have studied the
effects of school desegregation have recognized these benefits
as well. According to a veteran observer of these programs,
the distinguished sociologist and educator Amy Stuart Wells,
white children who go to schools that are racially diverse
"learn to address their own implicit biases in a way that can

help them think more clearly in the larger society. . . ." Critical thinking also tends to be enhanced when children with different vantage points are learning together in a classroom. And the natural friendships that are formed across the lines of class and race frequently endure well into their adult lives.

Question: The story about Julia Walker's oldest son, who rode the bus to Brookline and then, after college, became a teacher in the district, was particularly moving. What I found most fascinating was the way he was able, as you put it, to "wed" his love of music into racial history. I'd be curious, as a teacher, to know a little more about this. Was he also teaching the language arts, like other fourth grade teachers?

Answer: Yes, he was, but in his own original way. When I asked him about this, he explained that the unit he designed, which he called "The Mississippi Delta Blues," was, in part, an exploration of the metaphoric language that was often used by Black musicians before Emancipation, and in the Jim Crow years that followed, when more explicit language may have been too dangerous. The fourth grade children with whom he worked began to understand the uses and the power of connotative language, not only in the lyrics of the sorrow songs but also in the poetry to which he introduced them. So, while he was teaching history, he was also teaching language arts and wrapping it all together in the music he was playing.

I thought this was a wonderful example of what can happen when a gifted Black instructor in an integrated district is given the freedom to bring his own experience to bear in reaching into the language arts in a more inventive and, in this case, more culturally interesting and creative way than tends to be familiar in the standardized curricula.

Question: I think you told me once that one of Julia's daughters and other Metco students whom you knew when they were children also became teachers. But obviously, as you said, the recruitment of a former student to serve as a teacher in a district he or she attended is a very small step towards faculty diversity. Are you aware of any states or districts that have developed programs specifically intended to recruit more Black and Latino teachers?

Answer: One approach, which has been pioneered in a handful of cities and metro areas, is to create a college-level program that trains and certifies people of color who may already be working in a school, as paraprofessionals for instance, in order to bring them back to the school, no longer as part-time helpers, but as the classroom teacher. According to Bob Peterson, the former Milwaukee School Board member and editor of Rethinking Schools, Milwaukee has a homegrown program, known as "Grow Our Own," which is preparing Black and Latino teachers for the city's schools.

None of this, however, has yet to tilt the racial balance among counselors and teachers enough to make a visible difference in the nation as a whole. According to a book published in 2020, by Jesse Hagopian and Denisha Jones, titled *Black Lives Matter at School*, the numbers of Black teachers and counselors in American schools, far from increasing, have actually diminished over the course of recent years. Over the long run, I believe, it's going to take more than local efforts— I'm thinking also, for example, of a nationally funded system that offers strong incentives for faculty diversity—if we seriously intend to develop faculties that look a whole lot more like the children that they're serving.

Unhappily, in the wake of the ruling on affirmative action handed down by the Roberts court in July 2023, which will narrow the pipeline of college admissions for Black and Latino students, who might have chosen to go on and become teachers, any federal action to incentivize faculty diversity within the public schools is likely to continue to be highly limited, if it is not prohibited entirely, for a good long while to come. For now, it seems, the local districts will have no choice but to try even harder to find or grow their own.

Question: In making your arguments for inter-district integration programs such as Metco, you also recognize that, unless and until these kinds of programs are mightily expanded, the larger number of Black and Latino children will continue to attend the segregated schools within their own communities. Is it unrealistic to believe that some of those children may be able to enjoy anything like the relatively open-ended and fear-free education that is usually to be found in the less embattled and more progressive districts in the suburbs you've described?

Answer: Well, first of all, as I have said, there are plenty of principals and teachers in even the most racially isolated urban schools who do not buy into the disparate agenda and who do what they can to develop a more warm and less constraining atmosphere of learning. Knowledgeable parents can find these schools if they have the time and the navigation skills to track them down, and visit them, when they are making choices for their children. But most parents in the poorest and most deeply segregated sections of our cities seldom even hear about these schools or, if they do, often are too burdened with the pressures of their daily lives to track them down and work their way through the application processes while space is still available. They're not in the loop of the knowledgeable parents. Their children usually end up at the schools to which the city has assigned them, unless the parents are enticed to send them to a charter school.

This is why I've argued for the breaking down of district

lines far beyond the present scope of programs such as Metco. Metro-wide school districts, wherever this is feasible, would be an ultimate objective. For the children who remain in segregation, I place my faith in teachers who respect their students' human rights and human worth and have the courage to rage against a system that diminishes us all.

Question: In one of the earlier chapters of this book, when you began to speak of breaking down those district lines and enabling far more children of color to escape the present system of Jim Crow education altogether, I was surprised to see you use a word that is generally avoided by education writers. That word is "reparations."

The word, of course, has been used repeatedly by young Black people who protest in the streets, as well as older advocates and activists who share the sense of urgency and outrage that those young people voice—in reaction, for example, to the killing of George Floyd and the multitude of other killings we have witnessed by police. And historians and sociologists—and, sometimes, radical economists—often speak of reparations as a sweeping form of recompense for the injuries of slavery and decades of Jim Crow. But I very seldom hear that word in schools of education—and almost never among those who set and study education policy. I think there's a kind of dread of breaching the decorum that too often passes for civility in pedagogic circles.

Answer: Yes, I agree. But I think we need to find the nerve to interrupt that version of decorum. I think it's well past time to make good, at long last, on that "promissory note" that Dr. King described on the steps of the Lincoln Memorial in 1963. And, as I have argued in this book, one good way we can actually begin is by doing whatever it may take, and spending whatever it may cost, to break the back of the dual system that separates the children in our public schools. The dream that Dr. King repeatedly envisioned was not some kind of cloudy aspiration to be realized in a very distant future. "Now is the time," he memorably said, "to rise from the dark and desolate valley of segregation to the summit path of racial justice." Any attempt to dilute that dream is a betrayal of his legacy.

Bringing millions of our children across the lines of class and race in beautiful and culturally expansive and richly funded classrooms will, as we've seen, cost a vast amount of money, and, for those who are content with the system as it stands, it will cost much more than money: it will cost them the disruption of their shameful equanimity, their routine acquiescence in the suffering of other people's children.

Those who insist that there are less disruptive and less costly ways to raise the hopes and empower the success of children "over there" are simply blind to history. They're asking us to place our faith in another round of those same old cycles of reform within the bounds of segregation that have never worked before. They ask us to believe that apartheid education is perfectible.

There is no such thing as perfectible apartheid. It's all a grand delusion. I will say again what thousands of others—from Thurgood Marshall to Ted Shaw—have tirelessly told us so many times before. Separate is not equal. It never was. It isn't now. It won't be in another fifty years. Tests and punishments and scientific measurement and longer lists of incorrect behaviors are not going to "fix" it. Apartheid education isn't something you can "fix." It needs to be dismantled. How much longer will it be before enough good people who have "the best intentions" can summon up the ethical audacity to go beyond their good intentions and join us in the struggle to batter down those walls?

Acknowledgements

In the writing of this book, I have relied on the advice and drawn on the experience of a number of my closest friends and colleagues. I want to thank, first of all, my oldest friend in Boston, the indomitable Julia Walker, whom I first met in 1966 when we ran a Freedom School together and who continues today, at the age of ninety-one, to be a shrewd observer of the racial climate in this divided city. Thanks, too, to Julia's sons John and Phillip Walker and her kind granddaughter, Yolanda Walker, whose daughter, "Emily", is now completing high school in the Metco program.

Among the many colleagues who have helped to edit or revise various sections of this book, I want to thank Bob Peterson, John Merrow, Caroline Jalfin, Cathy Kalob, and the redoubtable Ted Shaw, who has generously taken time to write the foreword to this work. I also feel a special debt of gratitude to Lynn Nesbit, who has been my loyal literary agent for nearly forty years, and to my editors Diane Wachtell and Rachel Vega-DeCesario and the entire team at The New Press who have shepherded this book to publication.

I am also indebted to my patient friend and chief editorial assistant, Amy Ehntholt, who has worked with me from the inception of this book through its multiple revisions. With her steady hand and wise and cautious judgment, Amy has been an indispensable support in enabling me to bring this to completion.

I also want to thank Samantha Leder, a brilliant young researcher, now based in California, who has double-checked every item of public record in this book while she has also managed to uncover a wealth of data on virtually every school and district I've described. Her sister, Mindy Leder, has worked in tandem with Samantha and has also helped me to re-examine every note I've made in the course of classroom visits. And my thanks, too, to Emilia Cardona, who works here with me in my Cambridge office and has been my irreplaceable guide and editorial advisor throughout the often challenging process of production.

Finally, on a personal note, I want to thank a very close friend and colleague who has worked with me for decades. Cassie Schwerner first began to work with me in 1987 when I was beginning to pull together data for *Savage Inequalities*, which was finally published in 1991. Cassie, who is now the executive director of the Morningside Center for Teaching Social Responsibility in New York City, has continued to be my constant guide—and sometimes stubborn critic—throughout the writing of this book. I've been blessed for all these years to have her at my side.

Endnotes:

Sources, Documentation, Anecdotal Matter

vii EPIGRAPH: The lines from Langston Hughes are cited from his poem "Kids Who Die," written in 1938. See *The Collected Poems of Langston Hughes* (New York: Vintage Books, 1994).

Chapter 1. Two Degrees of Separation

3 SCHOOL SEGREGATION PRESENTLY AT HIGHEST LEVEL SINCE EARLY 1990S: Interviews with Ted Shaw, February 2023. Shaw is the former chief counsel for the NAACP/Legal Defense Fund. Among the major cases that he has tried were *Gratz v. Bollinger* (2003), in which the Supreme Court ruled in favor of Black and Latino students in an affirmative action suit against the University of Michigan. (The *Gratz* decision was reversed by the Roberts court in July 2023.) Shaw also litigated *Missouri v. Jenkins* (1995), a school desegregation case in which a court of appeals found the Kansas City, Missouri schools in violation of their obligation to provide equal education in a unitary system. Shaw is now director of the Center for Civil Rights at the University of North Carolina School of Law.

See also Gary Orfield, Erica Frankenberg, Jongyeon Ee, and Jennifer Ayscue, "Harming Our Common Future: America's Segregated Schools 65 Years After *Brown*," The Civil Rights Project, UCLA, May 10, 2019. I have also benefitted from the extensive writings, as well as the forceful advocacy, of University of Minnesota Law School professor Myron Orfield, who has worked to create a unified agenda to address the continuing disparities of race and class in segregated schools and neighborhoods.

4 CHILDREN OF COLOR "HAVE DIFFERENT WAYS OF LEARNING" AND REQUIRE DIFFERENT STRATEGIES: These beliefs, which were familiar in the Boston schools when I became a teacher almost sixty years ago, began to resurface in the 1980s and 1990s in writings, for example, like those of Charles Murray (*Losing Ground*, 1984, and *The Bell Curve*, 1994) and then in publications of The Heritage Foundation and other right-wing institutions. (See *No Excuses*, by Samuel Casey Carter, The Heritage Foundation, 2000.)

6 ERA OF EUGENICS: The movement dominated pedagogic thinking in the early 1900s, in part because it won the backing of prominent intellectuals, including psychologist Edward Thorndike, who argued in favor of "scientific

breeding" and the use of testing to determine capabilities for learning. His thinking contributed to the "scientific" theories of German intellectuals in the 1930s.

Chapter 2. Varieties of Tyranny

11 NUMBER OF PUBLIC SCHOOLS AND DIS-TRICTS: U.S. Department of Education, National Center for Education Statistics, Washington, DC, 2022.

11 "SCHOLAR POSITION," "ZERO TALK," ETC.: I first began to hear these terms in schools I visited more than fifteen years ago. They have since become more common. See, for example, the *New York Daily News*, March 29, 2014, and *Spectrum News NY1*, October 25, 2019.

11 "RED ZONE": See, for example, *The Philadelphia Inquirer*, May 3, 2018.

12 TEACHER IN LAWRENCE, MASSACHUSETTS, CITED: Amy Berard, a teacher at Guilmette Middle School, was quoted by Valerie Strauss in her blog, Answer Sheet, *The Washington Post*, July 25, 2015.

13 NO NONSENSE NURTURING: The widespread

use of the training program was described on the website of CT3 Education (Center for Transformative Teacher Training), 2020 and 2023.

13 "TWO-DAY TRAINING SESSION" FOR NNN IN TULSA, OKLAHOMA: *Tulsa World*, August 18, 2016.

14 "THERE ARE NO QUESTIONS": The words of the principal at the high school in New Haven were directed at the teachers of tenth grade students, according to *The Washington Post*, August 11, 2016.

14 THE SCRIPT INTENDED TO BE USED AT NEWLY FOUNDED CHARTER SCHOOL IN MASSACHUSETTS: "As part of its application to the state Board of Education, the charter school included a detailed hour-by-hour look at what a . . . typical school day will be like," according to the Massachusetts-based education podcast *Have You Heard*, December 7, 2012.

15 PUBLIC SCHOOL NEAR THE SOUTH LOOP OF CHICAGO: The enrollment of the school was eighty-nine percent Black and Latino in 2017 when I sat in on classes.

15 DOLLAR INCENTIVES, "BUYING BATH-

ROOM RIGHTS," ETC.: I visited the fourth grade class in Boston's South End in May 2019.

15 CHILDREN BEGAN TO STEAL FROM OTHERS WHO HAD MORE "EARNINGS" IN THEIR POUCHES: In another elementary school, this one in a Maryland district, where the dollars were known as "Wizard Bucks," a parent told me that her daughter "figured out the earnings system when she was still in kindergarten." By the time she was in second grade, she and a co-conspirator "had created a black market" to trade with other children who had earned fewer dollars. The practice of using simulated money to spur young children to compete with one another, she observed, is "directly linked" to practices encouraged by employers on the factory floor.

19 "ONE DEAD GOLDFISH": The former first grade teacher whose class I used to visit when she taught in Boston has since been working with younger teachers in the Washington, DC, area. Her name, like that of several other teachers cited in this book, has been disguised in order to protect her privacy.

21 LINDA NATHAN'S DECONSTRUCTION OF THE IMPACT OF THE "GRIT" AGENDA: *When Grit*

Isn't Enough (Boston: Beacon Press, 2017). Nathan is presently a lecturer on "school design and school observation" at the Harvard Graduate School of Education.

22 "GRIT," STILL A FAMILIAR TERM: According to *Chalkbeat Tennessee*, October 23, 2022, the deputy superintendent of the Shelby County, Tennessee, schools has stated, "Our students, they epitomize grit and grind. . . ."

22 ACADEMIC FIGURES WHO DEFEND THE GRIT AGENDA: One of the most prominent advocates for this approach is University of Pennsylvania professor of psychology Angela Duckworth, whose influential but controversial book, *Grit: The Power of Passion and Perseverance* (New York: Scribner, 2016), became a national bestseller on its publication. In a recent opinion piece in *Education Week* (September 20, 2023) Duckworth discusses what she believes to be familiar misunderstandings about grit on the part of many teachers.

22 "GROWTH MINDSET": *Mindset: The New Psychology of Success*, by Carol Dweck (New York: Penguin Random House, 2006). The themes of the book, which focus on personal and professional self-development, did not begin to infiltrate the world of school reform until some years later. See *Education Week*, September 10, 2013.

23 COMPLICATED HISTORY OF PETERSBURG, VIRGINIA: "Petersburg was one of the busiest slave markets in the old South, but it also had one of the highest concentrations of free Blacks . . . and Pocahontas Island was where many [freed slaves] went to live." (*The Washington Post*, September 26, 2016.) Petersburg was also known for its involvement in attempted slave rebellions, including the aborted rebellion known as Gabriel's Conspiracy in August 1800. A number of men from Petersburg also participated in the march that led to the raid on Harpers Ferry in 1859.

23 THE POPULATION PROSPERED FROM THE TOBACCO TRADE: See "1730–1935 Petersburg's Tobacco Industry," Historic Petersburg Foundation, 2019.

23 ROBERT E. LEE ELEMENTARY SCHOOL: I visited the school in May 2017 and was accompanied by the superintendent of the district, who candidly described the difficulty he was facing in staffing classes with permanent teachers.

26 NAME OF THE SCHOOL HAS BEEN CHANGED: Robert E. Lee Elementary School was renamed Lakemont Elementary in 2018.

26 PETERSBURG FISCALLY BANKRUPT AT TIME OF MY VISIT: The city has since emerged from bankruptcy, and its financial situation has apparently improved. (*The Progress-Index*, Petersburg, Virginia, June 21, 2022.)

26 PETERSBURG'S HISTORY OF FIGHTING AGAINST SERVITUDE: While I was in Petersburg, I also visited the Peabody Junior High School, a nearly seventy-year-old building that has since been closed—in which, however, I had a chance to watch a stunning African dance performance by a group of lively students under the direction of a brilliant dancer and choreographer, Kwame Shaka Opare. While they danced, one of the girls stepped forward on the stage and sang, in a clear and thrilling voice, "We shall not bow down. . . ." It was the most hopeful moment in the days I spent in Petersburg.

Chapter 3. Learned Helplessness

29 "THE FIRST GREAT LAW IS TO OBEY": "A Curriculum Guide in Character Education" was issued for the use of teachers in the Boston Public Schools in 1962. See *Death at an Early Age* (Boston: Houghton Mifflin, 1967).

30 MATCH EDUCATION MANUAL FOR "THE

DEMANDING TEACHER": I first grew aware of the document when it was cited by Valerie Strauss in her blog in *The Washington Post*, June 26, 2012. I subsequently located and printed the entire manual, from which I have drawn my description of the program.

32 NUMBERS ASSIGNED TO PERMISSIBLE LEVELS OF STUDENT CONVERSATION: See "The Silent Treatment: A Day in the Life of a Student in 'No Excuses' Land," aired on *Have You Heard*, December 7, 2012, cited above. The various levels of student conversation were elaborated in a handbook intended for the use of teachers.

33 SCHOOL IN DORCHESTER WITH LOCKDOWN ROOM IN HALLWAY: I visited the school, which is a privately managed public school, in November 2017. The school was operated by a group that also ran two charter schools in Boston and two others in Lawrence, Massachusetts. On a poster in one of the classrooms there was a drawing of a student sitting in what was described as "Scholar Ready" position. Arrows with various labels were pointing to different portions of the student's body. "Brain is thinking . . . Mouth is silent . . . Hands [are] locked . . . Feet on floor. . . ."

34 CHILDREN IN A TINY PADDED ROOM AT

A NEW YORK CITY SCHOOL: *New York Daily News*, December 11, 2013.

34 THIRTY-ONE STATES ALLOW SCHOOLCHIL-
DREN TO BE PLACED IN ISOLATION ROOMS: *Pro-
Publica Illinois* and the *Chicago Tribune*, November 19, 2019.
Sixteen of these thirty-one states permit this to be done to
children even when they pose no threat of danger to each
other or a teacher.

34 RACIAL DISPROPORTIONS IN USE OF ISO-
LATION ROOMS IN THE DISTRICT OF COLUMBIA
AND ELSEWHERE IN THE NATION: Solitary Watch,
January 20, 2020.

35 "CALM DOWN ROOMS," "REFLECTION
ROOMS," "QUIET ROOMS," "RELAXATION ROOMS":
CBS News, December 13, 2017. Also see *ProPublica Illinois*
and the *Chicago Tribune*, cited above.

35 CORPORAL PUNISHMENT ALLOWED IN
TWENTY-THREE STATES: According to data compiled
by the Education Commission of the States (August 2018),
nineteen states explicitly allow children to be beaten in their

schools. But four additional states (Idaho, Indiana, Kansas, and Connecticut) have enacted no prohibition on its use, which is left to the decision of a local school or district. The total of twenty-three states where children may be beaten is confirmed in *Education Week*, March 24, 2023.

35 BLACK CHILDREN AND CORPORAL PUN-ISHMENT: See "The Striking Outlier: The Persistent, Painful, Problematic Practice of Corporal Punishment in Schools," Southern Poverty Law Center and the Civil Rights Project at UCLA, 2019.

35 CORPORAL PUNISHMENT IN THE TEXAS EDUCATION CODE: Chapter 37 Discipline, Law and Order Section 37.0011, became part of the Education Code on September 1, 2011.

36 ELIZABETH GERSHOFF CITED: "Corporal Punishment in U.S. Public Schools: Prevalence, Disparities in Use, and Status and State and Federal Policy," *Sociology Policy Report*, September 1, 2016. In Pickens County, Alabama, according to Gershoff, the board of education mandates that schools use a "wooden paddle approximately 24 inches in length, 3 inches wide and 1/2 inch thick that does not have

holes, cracks, splinters, tape, or other foreign material when administering corporal punishment to students."

36 OTHER STIPULATIONS FOR INFLICTING CORPORAL PUNISHMENT: In Covington County, Mississippi, according to the Hechinger Report, June 6, 2022, there are rules about how many "licks" from a paddle a child can receive in a given day as well as the warning that refusal to accept corporal punishment may result in a suspension. In another instance, at a charter school in Richmond County, Georgia, according to *Time*, September 10, 2018, there were stipulations that an "adult witness" is present and that "no more than three licks should be given" to a child.

36 APPROXIMATELY 70,000 CHILDREN BEATEN IN THEIR SCHOOLS IN 2017–18: U.S. Department of Education, Civil Rights Division, 2017–18 State and National Estimates, and Hechinger Report, June 6, 2022.

37 CORPORAL PUNISHMENT OF STUDENTS NOT PROHIBITED UNDER EIGHTH AMENDMENT: *Ingraham v. Wright*, 430 U.S. 651 (1977). Justice Lewis Powell, who wrote the majority decision, had been appointed to the Supreme Court by President Nixon in 1971.

38 EIGHTEEN-YEAR-OLD BEATEN IN SAN ANTONIO: *The Schoolhouse Gate: Public Education, the Supreme Court, and the Battle for the American Mind*, by Justin Driver (New York: Penguin Random House, 2018).

38 FIVE-YEAR-OLD IN TEXAS: The kindergarten student who stuck his tongue out at a teacher began having nightmares after he was beaten at his school in Dallas County, Texas. (*VICE News*, October 9, 2017.)

38 SIX-YEAR-OLD DRAGGED OUT OF KINDER-GARTEN CLASS IN FLORIDA: A local television station released video footage of the boy being dragged through the hallway at his elementary school in Lake County, Florida. According to the news report, the child was "dragged like a little rag doll" by the school dean and another school official and then, as the school reported later, was "pushed down into a chair and choked." (*WESH 2*, April 21, 2021.)

39 EIGHTH GRADE GIRL PLACED IN CHOKE-HOLD IN HOLMES COUNTY, MISSISSIPPI: "Where Lynching Terrorized Black Americans, Corporal Punishment in Schools Lives On," by Rebecca Klein, *Huffington Post*, July 21, 2020.

39 "PHYSICAL PUNISHMENT OF BLACK BOD-IES": Aaron Kupchik, quoted by Rebecca Klein, cited above.

39 CORPORAL PUNISHMENT BELIEVED TO HAVE DECLINED IN COURSE OF RECENT YEARS: Brookings Institution, January 14, 2022; *Education Week*, March 24, 2023. But, as *Education Week* observes, schools and districts are likely to underreport the frequency of use.

39 CHILDREN OF COLOR MORE LIKELY THAN WHITE CHILDREN TO BE ARRESTED AT THEIR SCHOOLS: According to the U.S. Department of Education Office for Civil Rights, "School-Related Arrests and Referrals to Law Enforcement in 2017–2018," Black students were three times as likely as white children to be arrested at their schools.

40 SIX-YEAR-OLD KAIA ARRESTED AT A CHARTER SCHOOL IN FLORIDA: *Orlando Sentinel*, February 24, 2020; *The Guardian*, February 25, 2020; *The Washington Post*, February 26, 2020; *The New York Times*, February 27, 2020; *Insider*, March 17, 2021.

40 SIX-YEAR-OLD BOY HANDED OVER TO POLICE: *Orlando Sentinel*, September 25, 2020.

41 BILL ENACTED IN FLORIDA TO PROHIBIT ARRESTS OF CHILDREN SIX YEARS OLD OR YOUNGER: According to HB 7051 Section 985.031 (CH 2021-241), passed by the Florida legislature in 2021, "A child younger than seven years of age may not be arrested, charged, or adjudicated delinquent for a delinquent act or violation of law based on an act occurring before he or she reaches seven years of age, unless the violation of law is a forcible felony."

41 TWENTY-FIVE STATES WITH NO MINIMUM AGE FOR CHILD ARRESTS: These states include: Alabama, Arkansas, Georgia, Hawaii, Indiana, Illinois, Idaho, Iowa, Kentucky, Maine, Maryland, Michigan, Missouri, Montana, New Jersey, New Mexico, Ohio, Oklahoma, Oregon, Rhode Island, South Carolina, Tennessee, Virginia, West Virginia, and Wyoming. (National Public Radio, May 5, 2022.)

41 MASS ARRESTS OF CHILDREN AT A TEN-NESSEE PLAYGROUND: The children, who were students at an elementary school in Rutherford County, Tennessee, were arrested on April 15, 2016. The juvenile court judge in the case, Donna Scott Davenport, and the 1,500 illegal arrests that she had overseen were described in a story by *ProPublica* and Nashville Public Radio, October 8, 2021.

See also National Public Radio, October 12, 2021, and *Daily News Journal*, Murfreesboro, Tennessee, January 18, 2022.

42 BLACK GIRLS FAR MORE LIKELY TO BE ARRESTED AT SCHOOL THAN WHITE GIRLS: "Data Snapshot: 2017–2018, National Data on School Discipline by Race and Gender," Georgetown Law Center on Poverty and Inequality, 2020.

42 BLACK GIRLS ARE SEVEN TIMES AS LIKELY TO BE GIVEN MULTIPLE SCHOOL SUSPENSIONS: U.S. Department of Education, cited in *The New York Times*, October 1, 2020.

42 BLACK GIRLS PERCEIVED AS "MORE SUSPICIOUS": *The New York Times*, October 1, 2020.

Chapter 4. Ironies and Desolation

45 THE MARTIN LUTHER KING JR. K–8 SCHOOL: I visited this school on June 3, 2019. The poor performance of the school has been tracked by the Massachusetts Department of Elementary and Secondary Education. (*The Boston Globe*, September 24, 2019.)

45 NOT A PHYSICALLY INVITING PLACE: According to a school infrastructure initiative introduced by Mayor Michelle Wu in March 2023, the MLK K–8 is "nearly 90 years old, its building is in urgent need of repair, with several maintenance areas categorized as high priority." Repairs are presently slated to begin in 2024.

46 OTHER SCHOOLS IN BOSTON IN MORE SERIOUS DISREPAIR: *The Boston Globe*, December 7, 2019. The eleven-year-old girl cited by *The Globe* said that she avoided using the bathroom at her school because the sinks were broken and the floor and toilet seats were covered in urine. As recently as September 2023, *The Globe* observed that bathroom renovations had been completed at only eight out of eighty Boston schools that were described as "high priority" for replacement or repair. (*The Boston Globe*, September 17, 2023.)

47 HEATING AND COOLING PROBLEMS IN PUBLIC SCHOOLS: See, for example, *The Fresno Bee*, September 7, 2022; *NBC News*, August 30, 2022; *Truthout*, June 26, 2022. Over a hundred schools in Philadelphia lack air conditioning systems, according to *The Philadelphia Inquirer*, June 3, 2022, and students have been routinely sent home due to unsafe learning environments.

47 CONTINUING LACK OF FUNCTIONAL COOLING SYSTEMS: According to *The Boston Globe*, September 6, 2023, the failure of the city to repair or replace the cooling systems was turning children's classrooms into "veritable saunas."

48 FREEZING ROOMS IN BALTIMORE SCHOOLS: *CBS News*, January 20, 2018. Also see *The Baltimore Sun*, January 15, 2018.

48 "IT'S LIKE A WATERFALL COMING DOWN": Teacher at elementary school in Lee County, Virginia, cited by *The Roanoke Times*, January 20, 2018.

48 AVERAGE AGE OF AMERICAN SCHOOLS: *The Washington Post*, January 8, 2018, estimated the age of the average school to be forty-five years old, based on data from the U.S. Department of Education, 2014. According to CNN, September 18, 2022, the executive director of the National Council on School Facilities noted that the average age of a school building had increased to nearly fifty years.

48 UNSUCCESSFUL ATTEMPTS TO INCLUDE SCHOOL REPAIR AND CONSTRUCTION FUNDS IN FEDERAL INFRASTRUCTURE BILLS: White House

press announcement, "The Bipartisan Infrastructure Deal," November 6, 2021; *Education Week*, March 31, 2021 and October 29, 2021; *US News*, November 5, 2021.

50 DANGERS OF LEAD EXPOSURE TO YOUNG CHILDREN: "50 Years of Research Shows There Is No Safe Level of Childhood Lead Exposure," Pulitzer Center, June 16, 2022.

51 ENVIRONMENTAL HAZARDS IN DISTRICT OF COLUMBIA: Report on "Neurological and Behavioral Consequences [of lead exposure] for Youth in the District of Columbia," National Academy of Medicine, October 2017.

51 AVERAGE PUBLIC SCHOOL WAS BUILT BEFORE 1978: "Condition of America's Public School Facilities: 2012–2013," U.S. Department of Education, National Center for Education Statistics, March 2014.

51 LEAD HAZARDS IN PUBLIC SCHOOLS "PRETTY UNIVERSAL" IN OLDER NEIGHBOR-HOODS: Tamara Rubin, the executive director of Lead Safe America, was quoted in *Huffington Post*, September 8, 2014.

52 LEAD HAZARDS AND CHILDREN OF

COLOR: See "Populations at Risk: Childhood Lead Poisoning Prevention," Centers for Disease Control and Prevention, October 29, 2021. See also Healthline, February 7, 2022.

52 LEAD AND OTHER TOXINS ALSO FOUND IN SCHOOL DRINKING WATER: The New York City Department of Education found that almost a quarter of all schools, 391 in total, contained high levels of lead in their water (*New York Post*, September 15, 2018). In Detroit, at least 57 public schools found lead and/or copper in their drinking water (*CNN*, September 20, 2018). In Houston, eighty-four percent of schools were found to have lead in at least one water source. (*Houston Chronicle*, October 26, 2022.)

52 DANGEROUS CONDITIONS IN PHILADELPHIA SCHOOLS: *The Philadelphia Inquirer* ran the three-part series "Toxic City" beginning May 3, 2018. The first installment of the series, "DANGER: Learn at Your Own Risk," described the boy who swallowed lead paint at his desk.

53 HIGH LEAD LEVELS IN NEWARK, NJ: According to *The New York Times*, August 14, 2019, "Environmental and health advocates have criticized city officials for failing to adequately address a growing health threat that began [in

2016] when high lead levels were found in the drinking water at nearly half the city's sixty-seven schools, forcing some to shut down fountains and test thousands of children."

54 LEAD IN THE WATER IN BOSTON SCHOOLS: Water fountains at an elementary school in Dorchester and a K–8 school in Roxbury showed high lead levels, according to *The Boston Globe*, April 24, 2016. Parents were advised to arrange testing for their children on their own.

54 "IF YOU'RE THIRSTY . . . , YOU JUST DRINK IT": The student at a school in Prospect Heights, Brooklyn, was cited by the *New York Post*, September 15, 2018.

55 "NO ONE . . . DID THIS TO MY SON": The parent, who, I believe, was an adjunct professor, lived in Brooklyn at the time.

55 ECONOMIC RECESSION IN 1970S, CUTBACKS ON FUNDING FOR NYC SCHOOLS: *The New York Times*, June 21, 1976; *The Nation*, April 16, 2013; *The New York Times*, May 5, 2017.

56 ECONOMY BOOMING IN NEW YORK IN 1999: *CNN*, April 30, 1999; *Fortune*, December 5, 2014.

56 FUNDING FOR PUBLIC SCHOOL REPAIRS CUT BACK AGAIN IN THE RECESSION OF 2008: *Education Week*, October 10, 2008.

57 MORE THAN HALF OF BOSTON'S SCHOOLS BUILT EIGHTY OR MORE YEARS AGO: WGBH, public radio in Boston, September 16, 2020.

57 LAST SIGNIFICANT SCHOOL CONSTRUCTION IN BOSTON TOOK PLACE IN 1960S AND 1970S: *The Boston Globe*, March 1, 2017.

57 MARTY WALSH, CAMPAIGN PLEDGE IN 2013: *Education Week*, October 29, 2013. When running for re-election in 2017, Walsh again announced a plan to spend $1 billion over the course of ten years and focus on school construction and repair. (*The Boston Globe*, January 17, 2017.) The plan proposed "the construction, renovation or major transformation of twelve schools, to be completed or in progress by 2027." (Press release, Boston Public Schools, October 2018.)

57 "BOSTON SCHOOLS SHOULD BE FLUSH WITH CASH": "The disconnect between the city's prosperity and the state of its schools has baffled parents, teachers, and education advocates for years. . . . Boston's latest push for

more aid comes as lawmakers debate updating the state's outdated formula for calculating local school aid. The formula has failed to keep pace with inflation and consequently is underfunding education by $1 billion or more, according to multiple state reports." (*The Boston Globe*, January 26, 2019.)

58 BOSTON MAYOR MICHELLE WU ANNOUNCED PROPOSAL FOR SCHOOL CONSTRUCTION: In May of 2022, Mayor Wu made a commitment of $2 billion "to overhaul Boston's deteriorating school facilities, under an ambitious effort that would begin with fourteen new school buildings or major renovations." (*The Boston Globe*, May 12, 2022.)

Chapter 5. Models of the Possible

61 CYCLES OF REFORM: In his book *Addicted to Reform* (New York: The New Press, 2017), the longtime *PBS NewsHour* correspondent John Merrow has addressed this pattern at great length. The enactment of the No Child Left Behind Act in 2002, he writes, "triggered what became sixteen years of non-stop school reform, guided by 'no-nonsense corporate' principles. . . ." Perhaps the most comprehensive effort at educational reform since No Child Left Behind was the promulgation and adoption of the Common Core, which

greatly reduced the exposure of children to literary works in favor of non-fiction writing—manuals of technical instruction, for example. The program was developed with financial backing from the Gates Foundation and won the support of corporate leaders because of its emphasis on "useful" skills that would allegedly prepare young people for the roles they were expected to fill in the nation's marketplace. Today, nearly fifteen years since it began to be adopted, only eleven states continue to make use of the Common Core assessment (*Education Week*, August 2, 2022).

61 "OPERATION COUNTERPOISE": See *Death at an Early Age*, cited above.

63 SCHOOLHOUSE BULLY JOE CLARK: *The New York Times*, December 20, 2020. When I visited Eastside High in March 1990, I was told that two-thirds of the students Clark had expelled had landed in the Passaic County Jail.

63 WIDENING OF RACIAL GAP SINCE INTEGRATION EFFORTS WERE ABANDONED: According to Nikole Hannah-Jones, "By 1988 . . . school integration in the United States had reached its peak and the achievement gap between Black and white students was at its lowest point

since the government began collecting data. . . . As schools have since resegregated, the test-score gap has only grown." (*The New York Times*, June 9, 2016.)

64 PROMOTIONAL CAMPAIGNS FOR CHARTER SCHOOLS, FUNDING FROM CONSERVATIVE GROUPS AND INDIVIDUALS: *The Nation*, March 19, 2015; *The Washington Post*, December 1, 2021; *CNBC*, May 9, 2022. In Boston, for example, money from two of the Walton billionaires, among other wealthy donors, was used in an effort to win support for raising the cap on charter schools prior to a referendum that the voters, fortunately, rejected. See my opinion piece "Vote 'No' on Charter Schools," *The Boston Globe*, October 27, 2016.

64 CHARTER SCHOOLS HAVE TENDED TO BE BASTIONS OF RACIAL SEGREGATION: According to Gary Orfield, cited above, "We have run the data through the 2021–2022 school year" and this continues to be true. (Correspondence with Orfield, May 2023.) See also "How Charter Schools Are Prolonging Segregation," Brookings Institution, December 11, 2017.

65 UNCONCEDED SELECTIVITY IN CHARTER SCHOOL ENROLLMENT: "Yes, Some Charter Schools

Do Pick Their Students. It's Not a Myth," Answer Sheet, *The Washington Post*, January 21, 2021. A common form of selectivity is conditioning the enrollment of a child on ability or willingness of the child's parent, or parents, to participate in "required" volunteer activities. Then, too, if a student, once admitted, turns out to pose behavioral problems that the school did not anticipate, parents have been told their child would be better served at a different kind of school. See also "New York Charter Schools Write Their Own Rules . . ." *ProPublica*, May 23, 2023.

66 "INTEGRATION . . . THE ONE THING THAT REALLY WORKED": Nikole Hannah-Jones is cited from her interview with Ira Glass on the public radio program *This American Life*, July 31, 2015. Hannah-Jones has talked extensively about her own participation in a school busing program in Iowa and has examined a number of other busing programs. See, also, *The New York Times*, September 6, 2017 and July 12, 2019.

66 URBAN/SUBURBAN SCHOOL INTEGRATION IN ST. LOUIS: The voluntary inter-district choice program was begun in compliance with a federal appeals court order in 1981. I observed the program in two of the suburbs, Webster

Groves and Clayton, in 1985. John Ashcroft, Missouri attorney general and subsequently governor, termed the desegregation plan "plain wrong" and said he would repeal it. (*The New York Times*, February 9, 1984.) Despite his efforts, the program survived for more than forty years.

67 SCHEDULED TERMINATION OF ST. LOUIS PROGRAM IN 2024: *St. Louis Post-Dispatch*, February 18, 2022. According to the program's website, there will be no further extensions.

67 CROSS-DISTRICT INTEGRATION PROGRAM IN MILWAUKEE: "At its peak in the late '80s and early '90s, about 6,000 minority students and 1,000 white students participated" in the program known as Chapter 220. (WUWM Milwaukee public radio, February 18, 2019.)

67 BOB PETERSON CITED ON GOVERNOR WALKER'S OPPOSITION TO THE INTER-DISTRICT PLAN: Interview with Bob Peterson, January 2023.

67 "OTHER PROGRAMS...HAVE SURVIVED": Among these programs are those in the Hartford, Connecticut area, the Bay Area of California, and Rochester, New York. For

the current status of Hartford's Open Choice program, see the consent school desegregation plan to which the plaintiffs and the state of Connecticut agreed in 2022 as the final settlement the long-running case *Sheff v. O'Neill*. (Correspondence with former Sheff attorney John Brittain, April 18, 2023.)

67 METCO: At the time of writing, there are thirty-three suburban districts that participate in Metco. In order to enroll their children in the program, Boston families fill out applications and then await the outcome of a lottery. In any given year, only 350 to 450 enrollment slots open up for applicants. About two thirds of those who applied in the 2022–23 school year had to be turned away. (Interviews in January and February 2023 with Milly Arbaje-Thomas, who became executive director of Metco in 2018.)

68 ELLEN JACKSON, "OPERATION EXODUS," AND ORIGINS OF METCO: I first came to know Ellen Jackson at her storefront office in 1965 when I was teaching at the school I would later describe in *Death at an Early Age*. A fascinating article on "Operation Exodus" may still be found in the archives of *The Harvard Crimson*, October 18, 1965.

68 WAITING LISTS FOR METCO: The waiting lists

have now been officially abolished, for reasons that aren't clear to me, but parents still line up and wait for the outcome of a lottery in which they place their children's names.

69 MY FRIEND JULIA WALKER'S OLDEST SON: John Walker Jr. was already fourteen years old in the year when Metco started. He attended Brookline High School, where he did well academically. After college, where he studied art and music, he began to perform at local clubs and social events, until he was hired by the Brookline schools to work with children and their teachers at the elementary school where I observed his lessons.

70 "IT ISN'T ALWAYS PEACE AND JOY": In a book of interviews conducted in 1996 and 1997 with graduates of Metco, scholar and journalist Susan Eaton cited former students who said they had struggled to feel that they belonged in the schools they had attended, among other social and cultural challenges they faced. But they also spoke of the benefits they had gained and most of them said they would likely place their children in the program if they could. The book, which is titled *The Other Boston Busing Story* (New Haven: Yale University Press, 2001), gives a balanced picture of the experience of many Metco students more than a quarter-century ago.

70 MY ONE-YEAR TEACHING STINT IN BOS-
TON HAD ENDED PREMATURELY: The poetry of
Langston Hughes, I was told when I was fired, was inappro-
priate for children because he wrote in "dialect." (See *Death
at an Early Age*, cited above.)

70 TEACHING AT A METCO SCHOOL IN NEW-
TON: I taught at the Davis Elementary School, in an economically mixed community near West Newton Square,
from 1966 to 1968.

72 MY STUDENT'S MEMORY OF CLASSMATES
WHO DID NOT GO ON TO COLLEGE: Another stu-
dent from the class recently told me that she went off to Italy
after high school in order to study Renaissance art, instead of
attending college.

73 NUMBER OF STUDENTS IN SUBURBS THAT
PARTICIPATE IN METCO: Enrollment data for the
2022–23 school year, Massachusetts Department of Elementary and Secondary Education.

74 FUNDING FOR METCO BARELY ENOUGH
TO KEEP UP WITH PRESENT NEEDS: *The Boston
Globe*, March 18, 2022.

Chapter 6. Culture and Identity

77 UNWILLINGNESS OF CONGRESSIONAL LEADERS TO PROVIDE SUPPORT FOR RACIAL INTEGRATION IN THE PUBLIC SCHOOLS: There were two recent attempts by members of the House—one by former representative Marcia Fudge in 2020, the other by representative Bobby Scott in 2021—but both initiatives died in committee (Congress.gov).

78 PRESIDENT BIDEN'S OPPOSITION TO SCHOOL BUSING: Mr. Biden's interview in a Delaware newspaper in 1975 was cited by *The Washington Post*, June 27, 2019. Biden's letter to Mississippi senator James Eastland, expressing his thanks for Eastland's support of his anti-busing efforts, is dated June 30, 1997, according to *The Washington Post*, June 20, 2019. Biden was described as "the Anti-Busing Democrat" in a headline in *The New York Times*, June 15, 2019. During his electoral campaign in 2019 and 2020, Biden insisted, unconvincingly, that he had not opposed school integration—only the use of busing to achieve that goal—but he failed to explain why he had joined with Southern segregationists in their attempts to reverse the effects of *Brown v. Board of Education*. For additional information on Biden's willingness to ally himself with well-known Southern racists,

see my editorial in *The Nation*, July 6, 2019, "When Joe Biden Collaborated with Segregationists."

78 BIDEN INDICATES HE IS IN FAVOR OF FOSTERING DIVERSITY: In his initial fiscal year 2023 budget request, Biden proposed a modest sum of $100 million to "help communities voluntarily develop and implement strategies" promoting school diversity. (U.S. Department of Education, Fiscal Year 2023 Budget Summary.) In May 2023, a grant program to promote school integration was announced by the U.S. Department of Education, but the sum was only $10 million, "a small fraction" of the sum that the president had initially proposed. (*Chalkbeat*, May 18, 2023.) The sum was increased to $12.5 million in October of 2023, again according to Chalkbeat (October 19, 2023.)

80 INCREASING MEDIA SUPPORT IN BOSTON FOR CROSS-DISTRICT BUSING: *The Boston Globe*, February 17, 2019; June 20, 2022; December 5, 2022. See also public radio WBUR Boston, February 26, 2021, and WGBH Boston, October 6, 2021.

80 SCATHING STORIES OF PERSISTENT AND INCREASING RACIAL SEGREGATION IN BOSTON

SCHOOLS: *The Boston Globe*, August 4, 2018; June 20, 2020; December 11, 2020; April 1, 2021; April 6, 2021; June 2, 2021.

81 ARGUMENT FOR EXPANSION OF "EXTRAORDINARILY SUCCESSFUL . . . PROGRAM KNOWN AS METCO": David Scharfenberg, *The Boston Globe*, March 18, 2022.

81 METCO STUDENTS' GRADUATION RATES: Scharfenberg references a study by Harvard researcher Ann Mantil, which draws on state data in regard to Metco students.

81 PROPOSED LEGAL ACTION UNDER MASSACHUSETTS CONSTITUTION: Scharfenberg, cited above.

81 "ADEQUACY" CLAUSE IN MASSACHUSETTS CONSTITUTION: According to a ruling of the state's Supreme Judicial Court, there is "an affirmative duty on the Commonwealth to provide a level of education in the public schools for the children there enrolled that qualifies as constitutionally adequate." (Boston Bar Association, August 15, 2018.) Court rulings and/or constitutional provisions in many other states also require "adequate" levels of education for children in their public schools. But what is considered to be "adequate" is usually a matter of heated contestation.

82 DIRECTOR OF BOSTON-BASED LAWYERS FOR CIVIL RIGHTS: Iván Espinoza-Madrigal, cited by Scharfenberg in *The Boston Globe*, March 18, 2022.

83 EFFORTS TO RECRUIT MORE THAN TOKEN NUMBERS OF BLACK AND LATINO FACULTY AND COUNSELORS IN METCO SCHOOLS: According to Metco director Milly Arbaje-Thomas, "there is a concerted effort" to diversify "the staff in general" throughout the Metco districts. Some of the towns have used their Metco funding to reach out to Black counselors or social workers, for example. But the recruitment of Black and Latino teachers up to now has been far from sufficient.

84 TWO BOYS "DOING THE GREENSBORO MOVEMENT" AND CORRECTING MY POOR MEM-ORY IN FOURTH GRADE CLASS: I visited the school in Newton, Massachusetts, in the neighborhood where I grew up, in June 2017.

84 "CIVIL RIGHTS WAS ON THE MINDS OF OTHER CHILDREN AT THE SCHOOL": According to Arbaje-Thomas, cited above, none of this is left to chance. A broad array of anti-racist workshops, organized at the district

level, has been introduced, often as a requisite part of teacher preparation.

85 NINTH GRADE STUDENT FROM ANGOLA AT INTEGRATED SCHOOL IN VIRGINIA COL-LEGE TOWN: I visited the school and observed the diversity and successful integration of its students in September 2016.

Chapter 7. Education Without Fear

89 GAP IN SCORES REDUCED BY HALF WHEN INTEGRATION WAS ENFORCED: Nikole Hannah-Jones, interview with Ira Glass, cited above.

91 TEACHER AT SUCCESS ACADEMY RIPS CHILD'S PAPER: *The New York Times*, February 12, 2016.

92 "THERE MUST BE MISERY FELT": *The New York Times*, April 6, 2015.

94 CHILDREN BUILDING BRIDGE: I visited this integrated and child-friendly school in the fall semester of 2016.

96 VISITING CHILDREN IN THE BRONX WITH
FRED ROGERS: We visited an afterschool program at a
church in the Mott Haven neighborhood and talked with
children in kindergarten and first grade at a nearby school,
first in the fall of 1996 and again in the spring of 1997. I
described those visits in some detail in my book *Ordinary Resurrections* (New York: Crown, 2000).

Chapter 8. Batter Down the Walls

100 ADOLPH REED CITED ON "OBSESSION
WITH DISPARITIES OF RACE": *The New York Times*,
August 14, 2020. His reference to "a kind of luxuriation in
a romanticized fantasy of suffering" appeared in an interview
with *Jacobin*, March 5, 2022.

103 "NOW SEGREGATION SEEMS TO BE ALMOST
THE ORDER OF THE DAY": My conversation with Con-
gressman John Lewis took place in his Washington office in
September 2003.

105 "GOOD TROUBLE": After John Lewis passed,
Biden released the following statement: "And to John,
march on dear friend. May God bless you. May you reunite

with your beloved Lilian. And may you continue to inspire righteous good trouble down from the Heavens." The statement was posted on the digital platform *Medium*, July 18, 2020.

106 JOHN LEWIS VOTING RIGHTS ADVANCEMENT ACT, PASSED IN HOUSE, BLOCKED IN SENATE: *The New York Times*, November 2, 2021. Senate Democrats tried again to open debate and pass the act in January 2022 but could not break Republican resistance. (*The New York Times*, January 19, 2022.)

106 HAITIAN CHILDREN WHIPPED BACK INTO RIVER: *MSNBC*, September 20, 2021; *BBC News*, September 23, 2021; *CBS News*, July 8, 2022.

107 HAITIAN MIGRANTS SENT BACK TO HAITI ON PLANE FLIGHTS: "From January 1, 2021 through February 26, 2022, 25,765 people were returned to Haiti by plane or boat, including 4,674 children," according to Human Rights Watch, March 24, 2022. The Biden administration also expelled "nearly 4,000 Haitians on 36 deportation flights" in May 2022, according to *The New York Times*, June 9, 2022.

Chapter 9. A Letter to the Future

111 LOSS OF SCHOOL LIBRARIANS IN NEW YORK CITY BETWEEN 2005 AND 2022: *Education Week*, February 16, 2022. By 2023, "more than half the city's schools [lacked] a legally mandated full-time librarian, and two fifths lack a library," according to *Education Week*, February 27, 2023.

111 SCHOOL LIBRARIANS IN LOS ANGELES: Data from the U.S. Department of Education, National Center for Education Statistics, revealed that in the 2021–22 school year, there were 134 librarians serving 435,958 students in the Los Angeles Unified School District.

111 SCHOOL LIBRARIANS IN CHICAGO: *Chicago Sun-Times*, June 18, 2022.

112 SCHOOL LIBRARIANS IN CLEVELAND: U.S. Department of Education, National Center for Education Statistics, data for 2021–22 school year.

112 SCHOOL LIBRARIANS IN DETROIT: U.S. Department of Education, National Center for Education Statistics, data for 2021–22 school year.

112 SCHOOL LIBRARIANS IN BOSTON, CAM-BRIDGE, AND SUBURBAN NEWTON: U.S. Department of Education, National Center for Education Statistics, data for 2021–22 school year.

112 RACIAL AND ECONOMIC CLASS COMPOSITION OF STUDENT POPULATION IN SCHOOLS LEAST LIKELY TO HAVE LIBRARIANS: According to a report by the School Librarian Investigation, "the losses of school librarians [impacted] mostly non-white districts and districts with larger percentages of economically disadvantaged students. . . . Pandemic-related librarian losses were almost twice as likely to occur in majority Black districts as in other districts, the report found." (*Education Week*, April 17, 2023.) In Chicago, according to the *Chicago Sun-Times*, July 18, 2022, "As the impact of budget cuts hit schools along racial lines over the past decade, a disparity developed: There are librarians at only 10 percent of schools where Black students are the largest percentage of the student body."

113 "I WANT TO CHANGE THE FACE OF READING INSTRUCTION FROM AN ART TO A SCIENCE": Susan B. Neuman, assistant secretary of education for the U.S. Office of Elementary and Secondary Education, cited by *The New York Times*, January 9, 2002.

113 "SO MAYBE WE AREN'T TEACHING AN ENTIRE NOVEL": Kimberly Skillen, district administrator for secondary curriculum and instruction in Deer Park, New York, cited by *The New York Times*, June 19, 2015.

114 "HOKEY LITTLE BITS AND PIECES" OF TEST-ALIGNED MATERIALS: The teacher in Virginia vividly recalled the passages she was forced to use and the overwrought instructions that she thought were "gobbledygook." For the passage about the blobfish and examples of the other passages that took the place of reading books, see "Grade 5 Reading: 2010 English Standards of Learning," Virginia Department of Education, 2015.

118 THE FLIGHT OF TEACHERS NOTED AS A GROWING CRISIS: According to the nonprofit education news organization *The 74 Million*, in a survey released March 23, 2022, almost two thirds of the 100 largest urban districts were "struggling" to fill instructional positions. According to *Education Week*, March 4, 2022, "A national EdWeek Research Center survey, conducted in the fall, found that nearly half of district leaders and principals said they had struggled to hire a sufficient number of full-time teachers this school year. . . . Also, enrollment in teacher-preparation programs has been declining steadily over the past decade."

See also "People Don't Want to Be Teachers. Can You Blame Them?" In *The New York Times*, September 13, 2023.

118 LOW SCALE OF TEACHER PAY: According to data released by the U.S. Department of Education, National Center for Education Statistics, drawing on surveys conducted in the 2017–18 school year, cited by *Mother Jones*, March 30, 2022, "About 600,000 . . . public school teachers in the U.S. held second jobs outside the school system during the school year, making teachers about *three times as likely* as all U.S. workers to juggle multiple jobs at once." According to *Education Week*, August 22, 2022, "Teachers are paid less than their college-educated peers in other professions—a trend that's only getting worse over time . . . , according to a new analysis by the Economic Policy Institute, a nonpartisan think tank supported partially by teachers' unions." Also see *The New York Times*, October 6, 2022.

118 MEXICAN AMERICAN STUDIES PROGRAM IN TUCSON, ARIZONA: The program began in 1997 at the initiative of teachers in the Tucson Unified School District. In 2008, conservative lawmakers began to press for elimination of the program and, in 2012, Governor Jan Brewer signed a law that prohibited the program. (*News Taco*, January 21, 2012; *Politico*, July 11, 2021.) Since that time, according to

David Berliner, professor of educational psychology emeritus at Arizona State University, "The Mexican American Studies program has been restored—but not under that name—and not with so clear a mandate to review and remember the history of Mexican representation in the Southwest. . . . Its soul was gutted when the confiscations began years ago." (Correspondence with Berliner, February 17, 2023.)

119 FAR-RIGHT PARENT GROUPS LAUNCHING FIERCE ATTACKS: One of these groups, known as Moms for Liberty, is currently active in thirty-three states where it loudly harasses teachers and librarians. (*Newsweek*, November 3, 2022.). See also "Banned in the USA: The Growing Movement to Censor Books in Schools," by Jonathan Friedman and Nadine Farid Johnson, released by PEN America, September 19, 2022.

120 ERIC CARLE: See my citations from our correspondence in "A Tribute to Eric Carle," *The New York Times Book Review*, August 11, 2021.

Afterword: Author's Q and A

126 MORE THAN A MILLION ELIGIBLE CHILDREN UNABLE TO BE SERVED BY HEAD START

PROGRAMS: According to the Children's Defense Fund, March 18, 2019, "Despite serving over a million low-income children, fewer than half of eligible children [were] able to benefit from Head Start and less than 5 percent [from] Early Head Start."

126 CHILDREN UNSERVED BY STATE AND LOCAL PROGRAMS: Based on estimates from the National Institute for Early Education Research in "The State of Preschool 2021: State Preschool Yearbook," approximately 1,500,000 low-income children ages three to four years old were not enrolled in any preschool program in the 2020–21 school year.

126 COSTLY PRIVATE PRESCHOOL PROGRAMS: At the Little School in the Lower Pacific Heights neighborhood of San Francisco, preschool tuition in the 2023–24 school year was $34,000. At the Washington Market School in Lower Manhattan, preschool tuition was $44,900 for the 2023–24 school year. At the West Side Montessori School, also in New York City, the cost of a full-day preschool program in the 2023–24 school year was $54,000.

126 UNIVERSAL PRE-K PROMISED BY PRESIDENTIAL CANDIDATES: Barack Obama, Hillary Clinton, and

Joe Biden all promised universal pre-K on the campaign trail. (*The New York Times*, May 23, 2012; *Education Week*, June 15, 2015; *Chalkbeat*, June 13, 2019.)

127 ERIK ERIKSON, "DESTRUCTIVE CONSCIEN-TIOUSNESS": *Young Man Luther*, by Erik Erikson (New York: Norton, 1962).

127 PHONICS, "THE GREAT DEBATE": See, for example, "In the Fight Over How to Teach Reading, This Guru Makes a Major Retreat," *The New York Times*, May 22, 2022. For many decades, the opposition to highly structured phonics has been closely identified with Lucy Calkins, a professor of education at Columbia Teachers College. Calkins has recently revised the approach she recommends to include daily and sequential phonics instruction, but diehard phonics advocates do not forgive her for the balanced approach she has advocated in previous years. (*Education Week*, September 5, 2023.)

128 RESTORATIVE JUSTICE PRACTICES: Stop Bullying.gov, March 2, 2016; *Education Week*, January 9, 2020; *In These Times*, December 12, 2022.

128 HIGH CASELOADS FOR COUNSELORS IN ELEMENTARY SCHOOLS AND MIDDLE SCHOOLS:

"In grades K–8, the average ratio ranges from 613 students per counselor to 787 students per counselor," according to *Education Week*, January 5, 2023. As the American School Counselor Association has reported, there were only 120,793 school counselors to support more than 49,000,000 students nationwide in the 2021–22 school year.

128 "TRAUMA-INFORMED APPROACHES" SOME-TIMES REGARDED BY CRITICS AS OVERLY INDUL-GENT: But, according to the Hechinger Report, January 25, 2017, "Research to date shows that most—maybe 80 percent—of children who have trauma histories will thrive in a trauma-informed environment without further interventions."

129 COLORADO TEACHER CITED CONCERN-ING RESTORATIVE JUSTICE: I attended a "professional learning" conference at the teacher's school in the San Luis Valley, Colorado, in January 2018.

129 EDUCATION SECRETARY MIGUEL CAR-DONA CALLS FOR AN END TO THE USE OF COR-PORAL PUNISHMENT: According to *Education Week*, March 24, 2023, "Cardona urged districts and states to 'move swiftly toward condemning and eliminating' physical punishment for students."

131 VOCATIONAL AND JOB-SPECIFIC EDUCATION: "Urban school districts across the country have increasingly embraced career and technical education programs," according to *Chalkbeat New York*, March 20, 2023. *Chalkbeat* notes that New York City Schools Chancellor David Banks has made career preparation "one of the 'North Stars' of his administration."

132 LEAD-INFESTED WATER IN CALIFORNIA SCHOOLS: California Public Interest Research Group, August 19, 2020; *The San Fernando Valley Sun*, March 8, 2023.

132 LEAD IN WATER IN PHILADELPHIA SCHOOLS: Pennsylvania Public Interest Research Group, cited by WHYY Philadelphia public radio, February 16, 2022.

132 LEAD IN WATER IN TENNESSEE SCHOOLS: *Chalkbeat Tennessee*, August 29, 2019.

133 "DETERIORATING" LEAD PAINT IN "NEARLY 1,000 CLASSROOMS SERVING [NEW YORK'S] YOUNGEST STUDENTS": *Chalkbeat New York*, August 1, 2019.

133 BENEFITS OF INTEGRATION TO CHILDREN

IN PREDOMINANTLY WHITE COMMUNITIES: Teachers College professor Amy Stuart Wells is cited from her lecture "The Potential Educational Benefits of Diversity," presented at a forum hosted by the American Educational Research Association, in Washington, DC, April 9, 2016.

134 "THE MISSISSIPPI DELTA BLUES" AND AN INTRODUCTION TO CONNOTATIVE LANGUAGE: Conversations with Mr. Walker after my visit to his class and again in the winter of 2023.

135 ATTEMPTS TO ACHIEVE FACULTY DIVER-SITY BY EFFORTS SIMILAR TO "GROW OUR OWN": *Education Week*, June 8, 2021; National Education Policy Center, March 20, 2022; *Chalkbeat Philadelphia*, November 1, 2022.

136 RECENT DECLINE IN NUMBERS OF BLACK TEACHERS: *Black Lives Matter at School: An Uprising for Educational Justice*, by Jesse Hagopian and Denisha Jones (Chicago: Haymarket Books, 2020).

136 FACULTY DIVERSITY: The challenge is not only to recruit larger numbers of Black and Latino teachers and counselors, but to retain the teachers that we hire. See the

recommendations of the Center for Black Educator Development, cited by *Education Week*, March 23, 2023.

136 AFFIRMATIVE ACTION RULING HANDED DOWN BY ROBERTS COURT: *Students for Fair Admissions, Inc. v. President and Fellows of Harvard College* and *Students for Fair Admissions, Inc. v. the University of North Carolina* (June 29, 2023).

139 THE "PROMISSORY NOTE": Dr. King's words are cited from his speech, "I Have a Dream," delivered at the Lincoln Memorial in Washington, DC, August 28, 1963.

139 "NOW IS THE TIME": Dr. King's reference to "the dark and desolate valley of segregation" is also cited from "I Have a Dream."

Index

federal infrastructure bills, 48–9,
164–5n
Florida
children of color arrested in
schools, 40–1, 42, 161n
corporal punishment in
schools, 35, 38–9, 159n
Lake County, 159n
and state bill to prohibit arrests
of children six or younger,
161n
Floyd, George, 138
Frankenberg, Erica, 148n
Freire, Paulo, 119
Friedman, Jonathan, 188n
Frost, Robert, 72
Fudge, Marcia, 177n

Gabriel's Conspiracy (1800),
153n
Gates Foundation, 170n
Georgetown Law Center on
Poverty and Inequality, 42,
162n
Georgia
corporal punishment in
schools, 158n
no minimum age for child
arrests, 161n
Richmond County, 158n

Gershoff, Elizabeth, 36, 157–8n
Giovanni, Nikki, 117–18
Glass, Ira, 172n, 181n
Grandma's Purse
(Brantley-Newton), 120,
127
Gratz v. Bollinger (2003), 147n
Greensboro movement, 84, 180n
"grit" agenda, 21–3, 151–2n
*Grit: The Power of Passion and
Perseverance* (Duckworth),
152n
The Grouchy Ladybug (Carle),
128
"growth mindset," 22, 152n
Gulliver's Travels (Swift), 120

Hagopian, Jesse, 136, 193n
Haitian refugees, 106–7, 183n
Hannah-Jones, Nikole
on the racial achievement gap,
63–4, 89, 170–1n, 181n
on school integration, 65–6,
172n
Harpers Ferry raid (1859), 153n
Harriet the Spy (Fitzhugh), 120
Have You Heard (podcast), 150n,
155n
Hawaii: no minimum age for
child arrests, 161n

Head Start, 21, 126, 188–9n

Healthline: on lead poisoning, 52, 165–6n

heating and cooling problems in public schools, 47–8, 163–4n. *See also* school buildings in disrepair

Hechinger Report
 on corporal punishment, 36–7, 158n
 on trauma-informed approaches, 191n

Henkes, Kevin, 127

Heritage Foundation, 148n

Huffington Post
 on corporal punishment in schools, 39, 159n
 on lead hazards n schools, 165n

Hughes, Langston, xvii, 70, 72, 147n, 176n

humanities instruction, retreat from, 111–21, 130–1. *See also* language arts

Human Rights Watch: on Haitian migrants, 183n

Idaho
 corporal punishment in schools, 35, 157n

no minimum age for child arrests, 161n

"I Have a Dream" (1963 Martin Luther King, Jr. speech), 139, 194n

Illinois
 no minimum age for child arrests, 161n
 school librarians in Chicago, 111–12, 185n
 schools in Chicago, 15, 111–12, 185n

immigration policies, 106–7, 183n. *See also* Haitian refugees

Indiana
 corporal punishment in schools, 35, 157n
 no minimum age for child arrests, 161n

Ingraham v. Wright (1977), xiv, 37, 158n

integrated schools, xvi–xvii
 benefits for white children, 81, 133–4
 Hannah-Jones, 65–6, 172n
 inter-district programs, xvi–xvii, 66–74, 172–6n
 John Lewis on post-*Brown* schools, 102–5

About the Author

Jonathan Kozol's widely honored books include *Savage Inequalities, Amazing Grace, The Shame of the Nation,* and *Rachel and Her Children: Homeless Families in America.* He lives in Cambridge, Massachusetts.

Publishing in the Public Interest

Thank you for reading this book published by The New Press; we hope you enjoyed it. New Press books and authors play a crucial role in sparking conversations about the key political and social issues of our day.

We hope that you will stay in touch with us. Here are a few ways to keep up to date with our books, events, and the issues we cover:

- Sign up at www.thenewpress.com/subscribe to receive updates on New Press authors and issues and to be notified about local events
- www.facebook.com/newpressbooks
- www.twitter.com/thenewpress
- www.instagram.com/thenewpress

Please consider buying New Press books not only for yourself, but also for friends and family and to donate to schools, libraries, community centers, prison libraries, and other organizations involved with the issues our authors write about.

The New Press is a 501(c)(3) nonprofit organization; if you wish to support our work with a tax-deductible gift please visit www.thenewpress.com/donate or use the QR code below.